WORLD'S GREATEST
FLYFISHING
LOCATIONS

CRESENT BOOKS

New York

WORLD'S GREATEST
FLYFISHING
LOCATIONS

CRESENT BOOKS

New York

WORLD'S GREATEST FLYFISHING LOCATIONS

WORLD'S GREATEST FLYFISHING LOCA-TIONS has been originated, designed and produced by AB Nordbok, Gothenburg, Sweden.

Chief editor: Göran Cederberg
Graphic design: Thommy Gustavsson
Illustrator: Thommy Gustavsson
Translator: Jon van Leuven

World copyright © 1991, AB Nordbok, Box 7095, 402 32 Gothenburg, Sweden.

This 1991 edition published by Crescent Books, distributed by Outlet Book Company, Inc., a Random House Company, 225 Park Avenue South, New York, New York 10003.

Printed and bound in Spain

ISBN 0-517-05886-3

8 7 6 5 4 3 2 1

Photography

Johnny Albertsson: pages 38-39, 41.
Clayne Baker: pages 95-97, 118-125, 127.
Erwin Bauer: pages 3, 5, 87-89, 99-101, 103-109, 136-139.
Lennart Bergqvist: pages 25-27.
Göran Cederberg: pages 43-45, 55.
Mikael Frödin: pages 33-35, 56-57.
Roland Holmberg: pages 149-151.
Dave Hughes: pages 91-93, 111-113, 115-117, 129-131, 133-135.
Kristina Jansson: pages 21-23.
Jan Johansson: page 20.
Curt Johansson: page 33.
Jens Ploug Hansen: pages 12-15, 29-31, 66-69, 83, 157-159, 161-163.
Steen Larsen: pages 144-147, 153-155.
Benny Lindgren: pages 51-53, 63-65.
Arthur Oglesby: pages 6, 17-19.
Jan Olsson: pages 141-143.
John Roberts: pages 9-11.
Risto Seppänen: pages 59-61.
Steen Ulnits: pages 71-77, 82, 84-85.
Gunnar Westrin: pages 46-49, 78-81.

Contents

Preface

There is undeniably much more to flyfishing than the sheer delight of catching big fish. This sport provides superb experience of nature, and a fascinating opportunity to perfect one's casting techniques. It also yields the satisfaction of seeing a fish rise to a well-presented dry fly, and of finally discovering an imitation insect that even the most selective fish will approve of.

Many more reasons could be given for why a true flyfishing enthusiast is ready for great sacrifices in order to pursue the sport wholeheartedly. Here, in short, is a pastime that amounts to more than the sum of its parts. But a very important part is the place where one fishes, and each flyfisherman—or woman—has a personal favourite among the "dream waters" that he or she has visited or heard of.

For some of us, a great flyfishing location is our own little corner of the world, in which we can retreat to enjoy fishing and its atmosphere of nature and freedom. Such sportsmen seldom measure their experience in terms of kilograms and centimetres caught. Yet for others, dream water means an impressive environment, huge fish, long rushes against the leader, and perhaps a trophy to take home. These fishermen regard the end as more significant than the means—and the goal of a trip, quite often, as worth the effort in getting there.

Whichever category we belong to, it is generally the case that we find flyfishing pleasant, and all the more pleasant when we catch not only fish, but sizeable fish. Certain waters are relatively ideal for the sport, due to a variety of factors. Thus an overview of the world's best flyfishing waters must be something of a compromise—between different types of water, diverse surroundings, contrasting species and, in particular, individual habits and tastes. How a human being associates with the fish in the water he or she wets a fly in, as we know, is a highly personal matter.

The forty dream waters presented in this book are, nonetheless, similar in that they offer excellent fishing at times, their fish are both abundant and large, their environments are frequently of unique beauty, and they have long been reputed to reward visitors with unusually memorable experiences. This is not, of course, to give any guarantee that a fish will be caught on schedule.

While these waters are rightly ranked among the world's best, some of them are unfortunately difficult to reach, and must remain an unrealizable dream for the majority of flyfishermen. Most, however, are fairly open to any serious practitioner. It is hoped that the following pages will add a dimension of desire and do-it-yourself to the horizons of both beginners and experts at flyfishing. The attentive reader can hardly resist being drawn to new destinations and adventures that bring out the rough romantic in us all ...

Göran Cederberg

The Itchen

Lars-Åke Olsson

Winchester, an old capital of England, divides the Itchen into an upper and a lower stretch. This stream is 50 kilometres (30 miles) long, and flows through the attractive park-like landscape of southern England. At most places it is narrow and shallow, with a network of small irrigation channels and tributaries. The water is crystal-clear and runs over bottoms of gravel and loose chalk or limestone. Its vegetation is lush and, in common with most of the region's streams, there is plenty of insect life.

Trout and grayling

Such "chalk streams" flow over the expansive limestone base which can be found a foot or so under the thin soil cover on land. The water is constantly filtered through weeds that grow in the streams, explaining its clarity. Further, the grass provides protection to fish—as well as to nymphs, larvae and shrimp—and it helps to support the water level. At regular intervals, 3-5 times in a season, the grass is cut to prevent the streams from choking up and making it impossible to fish. Thresholds of grass are left, separated by open stretches of water. The cutters cooperate to remove weed during a single day along the entire valley, and the water becomes coloured by clumps of weed drifting about on it. In spite of this, one can fish as usual, though perhaps with somewhat poorer results. The water flow in the streams is also controlled by a series of dams.

Subdividing the Itchen are numerous stretches that belong to water-owners or are rented by clubs. Fish are set out at some of these places, but not at others which, consequently, have only wild trout and grayling. The grayling weigh up to a kilogram or so, and an attempt is made to keep them in check, as they multiply easily and can crowd out the trout. A fair share of fishermen, nonetheless, enjoy grayling at the times when trout are hard to catch, and during the autumn when trout fishing is over.

The trout weigh on average 0.6-1.5 kilograms (1.3-3.3 pounds), depending on which part of the river they come from. It is permitted to keep 2-4 fish, the number also varying with the stretch in question.

Correct presentation

The fishing season is from the beginning of April until the end of October. On the Itchen, and for that matter along most streams in southern England, a fishing day commences with the "morning rise" at ten o'clock. The fish start rising for newly hatched duns, which drift with the current—or for hawthorn flies, which are abundant in these waters and, during the early season, are as characteristic as the mayflies.

Moving upstream, the flyfisherman stays a little way from the bank's edge, watching for fish that rise, or for those that eat nymphs or shrimps underwater. Only the fish that can be seen rising are cast at. By two o'clock, the hatching may be finished, so that the fish stop eating and are much harder to take. But between 7:30 and 10:00 in the evening, the morning duns return in the form of spinners. After mating and laying eggs, they are "spent" and fall onto the water surface, dying or dead.

At the same time, sedge flies appear—either hatching or laying eggs, depending on which part of the season one is fishing in. They make it interesting to fish in the evening, and a simultaneous hatching of mayflies is not uncommon either. The form of rise shows whether the fish take a fast sedge fly, or a mayfly in the dun stage about to lift from the surface, or whether it slowly picks off a dead mayfly.

Your first two or three casts are important, for the manner of presenting the fly is crucial, even more so than your fly pattern. Thus it is worth casting softly and accurately, with more attention to your technique than to the choice of fly. Still, a flyfisherman must also be able to tell whether the fish is eating from or just beneath the water surface, and whether it is eating nymphs, newly hatched mayflies or sedge-fly pupae.

Reliable dry-fly patterns for the early summer are Itchen Olive, Gold Ribbed Hare's Ear, the large Dark Olive, Greenwell's Glory, Iron Blue Dun and Kite's Imperial—to name only some of the useful flies for fish that are taking mayfly duns. Others such as Hawthorn, Black Midge and Black Gnat represent the many tiny black bugs that live on the water throughout the season.

Good nymph patterns are the Itchen Olive, Pheasant Tail and Grey Goose. For fishing in high summer and autumn, the dry flies should be supplemented with B.W.O., Medium Olive and Blue Dun. Sedge-fly imitations in various sizes and colours, such as Skues' Little Red Sedge and Brown Sedge, should also be brought along—as well as imitations of sedge-fly pupae.

There are plenty of shrimp in the Itchen, too. As they are gladly eaten by the fish, some imitations of them also ought to be in the fisherman's fly box. Flies that resemble spinners are famous patterns such

The Itchen has several different species of fish, but its classic reputation is due to the unparalleled flyfishing for trout.

as Lunn's Particular, Houghton Ruby, Sherry Spinner and Red Spinner.

Interesting history

Winding through the green countryside about Winchester, the Itchen ranks as one of the finest fly-fishing streams in the world. This is not only because of its clear water, its well-grown and beautiful trout, and the teeming insect life. Equal thanks are due to its fascinating past, in which the personality of G. E. M. Skues and the origins of nymph fishing

played a leading role.

Skues avoided copying natural insects in great detail. He tied flies that represented them in form, size and colour. Then he fished the imitations upstream of rising fish, or fish that ate just under the water surface. In his view, the new method of wet-fly fishing should have a place alongside dry-fly fishing in the chalk streams—especially during periods when flying insects were scarce and the fish took nymphs, larvae and shrimp under the surface.

In 1910, Skues published *Minor Tactics of the Chalk Stream,* dealing with upstream wet-fly fishing. By then, dry-fly fishing had long dominated the chalk streams of southern England. His books and articles thus opened a fresh chapter in flyfishing history. Wet flies were "rediscovered", nymph fishing was born on the same waterways, and Skues became known as its father.

For more than 56 years, he fished the Itchen along a stretch called Abbots Barton. During this time he proved that wet flies were useful even in the clearest streams, and with the shyest fish—and that upstream wet-fly or nymph fishing is as difficult and demanding as dry-fly fishing.

So the Itchen is more than a stream which can still offer experiences beyond the ordinary. Its chronicles abound with curious, exciting events, eternally allied to Skues and the invention of yet another successful means of catching fish. ᴁ

Lough Corrib

Jens Ploug Hansen

Lough Corrib has no counterpart in the whole of Europe. This is the continent's largest fishing water for trout and salmon at no cost. A typical limestone lake, it has won fame for flyfishing in May. In addition, it offers dapping and blowline fishing in August and September, with natural crane-flies or grasshoppers on small hooks, using rods 14-16 feet long. A few years ago, there were around 700 boats on the lake's 45 kilometres (28 miles) of length in the beautiful, violet-coloured Connemara. Today the boats are less numerous, but the fishing is certainly no worse.

Flyfishing has a very old history on Lough Corrib. Yet only at the beginning of our century did foreign visitors turn their attention to this impressive, crystal-clear lake. At a meeting in Galway on June 18, 1898, the Corrib Fisheries Association was founded, with the aim of supporting both professional and sporting fishermen. A couple of years later, a similar society was formed.

During a meeting in 1908 at the Angler's Hotel in Oughterard, the associations proposed that trout should be bred and set out. Thereafter, the fishing improved considerably and won more recognition abroad. With the Irish struggle for independence, however, the organization of fishing declined. In 1951, the Inland Fisheries Trust arose, and its work has been invaluable for the lake's fine stocks of fish, whose gene pool has in fact never been diluted. There are only genuine wild trout in Lough Corrib, managed today by the Central Fisheries Board.

Trout in Lough Corrib weigh, on average, just under 1 kg (2.2 lbs).

Year round on Corrib

In March, the midges hatch and the fishing, consequently, is done with small black flies. Shortly afterward come the larger midges, and this "Duck Fly" season is a local phenomenon on Lough Corrib. Renowned for their Duck Fly fishing are Kitten's Bay, Inchiquin Bay, and Curra. In general, small wet flies of the Grey Duster type are fine all through April, when the big lake olives (*Cloeon simile)* hatch. At the beginning of May, the first mayflies are seen. The season reaches its peak around May 18-24, starting in the southern part of the lake and proceeding north for 7-10 days. The local inhabitants are predictably aware of the best spots—Doorus, Snaulauns, Kitten's Bay, Bog Bay, Ard, Faddas, Rabbit Island and others—where the trout run wild among all the delicacies.

Much of the mayfly fishing is still done with live natural insects. These are collected by schoolchildren and sold to eager flyfishermen, who keep the naturals in special bags.

An average catch contains 5-6 trout weighing 700-800 grams each, and 10-12 fish are reckoned to be a good day's catch. Now and then, rich yields of 20-30 trout occur before nightfall. It follows that a lot of "food fishermen" operate on Lough Corrib at this time. After the mayfly season comes a calm period, when the trout are hard to tempt because their favourite meal consists of perch fry.

During August and September, caddis-fly fishing can be hectic. The insects hatching are *Phryganea (varia, obsoleta)*, called "Peters" on Lough Corrib. This is the crane-fly and grasshopper season, ripe for dapping and blowline fishing. Tourists usually fish with artificial imitations of these big insects, but nearly all of the locals are faithful to the live originals. They are fished on rods 14-16 feet long, and the line must be light in order to be taken well by the wind. A few older fishermen still prefer lines made of floss silk, and leaders made with a mixture of floss silk and nylon, so that the wind will grab the fine silk fibres. The fly really must dance on the waves, while drifting away in the characteristic "slicks" of foam that appear when the wind blows against promontories and reefs, creating wakes that are hundreds of metres long. Despite all the billowing foam and water, these slicks are like oil on the surface, attracting trout to feast on grasshoppers and crane-flies. The crane-fly imitations, or "daddy-long-legs", are popularly termed "Harry" and used for "Harry-fishing".

Trout of 4-5 kilograms

One need not go far into Oughterard, on the west side of Lough Corrib, before noticing that the village is completely occupied with the lake's fishing. Here the beer is poured in pitcherfuls at the May Fly Inn, and Old Irish gilds the glasses. Old boatsmen and gillies still gather, and record-size trout shine from pedestals in the glow of century-old chandeliers. Fishing talk can easily be heard in the smoky cabins. At some of the pubs, there are pictures and sketches by traditional Englishmen in Harris Tweeds, with mustaches from the colonial era, alongside jolly scenes from archives and local history showing fishermen with greenheart rods and antique Hardy reels. Corrib must have been a very lively place in the old days. But the conflict in Northern Ireland persuaded English flyfishermen to stay home—while their Continental colleagues are much less enthusiastic about trout than the Irish tend to believe, and prefer instead to catch pike or perch, which abound in Corrib. It has yielded some of the biggest pike in Europe, one of them having reputedly weighed 30 kilograms (66 pounds).

The trout, too, can reach considerable sizes. Every year, trout of 3-4 kg (6.6-8.8 lbs) are landed, especially during the mayfly season, even if this is exceptional. When the trout begin to attain weights of 0.5-1 kg (1-2 lbs), and to eat perch fry, it is not long before they become cannibals—and once on a trout diet, they grow incredibly fast. A good number of trout in the 10-12 kg (22-26 lbs) range have been caught on spoons in this great lake. So the chances are still good, though the old boatsmen are no longer active. One hardly finds full-time gillies, yet only 10-15 years ago they did exist: among others, the legendary Tom Kyne in Oughterard.

Fishing spots

Both boatsmen and advice can be found at many places, such as Portacarron, Oughterard, Baurisheen, Derrymoyle, Cong, Greenfields, Doorus, Carrick and Carrey's. The Central Fisheries Board—together with Peter O'Reilly, a biological assistant and capable flytier—has published an excellent map with drawings of all fishing spots in Lough Corrib, as well as other interesting information about the lake. Yet one cannot manage without a guide's help for a half or whole day. His local knowledge will save many weeks of trouble and toil in studying the lake, letting you ride on the waves of adventure in the hands of an old fox. There are many fine places to

start from, but personally I am most fond of Oughterard, the very soul of Corrib fishing. ⁊

Lakeland is a boarding-house in Portacarron, a mile or two south of Oughterard. It offers first-class sportfishing service, including boat guides and boats. Renting boats is seldom difficult, but during the mayfly season they should be booked 2-3 months in advance. The address is: Lal & Mary Faherty, Lakeland, Portacarron, Oughterard, County Galway.

The River Spey

Arthur Oglesby

Some say the Spey is a river which separates the men from the boys. It does not yield its trophies too easily or to those who have not become acquainted with it. The Spey responds best to the deep-wading angler who can throw a long line and is more content to fish the fly—with either a sinking or floating line—than merely spinning.

As one of the four prime salmon rivers in Britain, the Spey has enjoyed a long and chequered history as a highly valued sporting resource. Much of its angling history relates to the period after railways reached the Scottish Highlands in the mid-nineteenth century. Previously only local residents could fish in this river. And before the mid-eighteenth century, when Scottish clans were still raiding each other's territory, you would have needed a whole army to fight your way to Strathspey.

Salmon fishing, still in its infancy as a sport at that time, was pursued mainly by commercial netsmen on behalf of those who owned the land or fishing rights. But there are now many proprietors, and most open their water to tenants for prices that depend on the sporting potential.

Early rising

The river rises in Loch Spey in Inverness-shire. With a drainage area of 1,097 square miles (2,840 sq. km), it is the next largest river in Scotland. After a run of almost 100 miles (160 km), it empties into the sea at Spey Bay. It relies heavily on winter snowfall on the nearby Cairngorm Mountains, which tends to melt in April-May and bring the Spey to a good level for the main spring run to enter. Yet only the severest winter prevents a few fresh fish from being as far upstream as Grantown on February 11, the opening day.

The main build-up of spring fish—unfortunately few in recent years—comes in late April and May. Then, depending on rainfall, the river should get good stocks of summer-run fish during late June, July and August.

It is impossible to state clear rules about the salmon fishing. In some years the spring run has made directly for the middle reaches, where in 1978 the anglers caught 207 salmon—all on the fly—in one May week on the Castle Grant water alone. Such catches are not common, but the Spey does hold fresh fish throughout the season, even though the middle and upper reaches mostly yield fish that have been in the river a long time as the season wanes.

While the Spey is not noted for record-size fish, specimens of 50 lbs (23 kg) were caught by net and rod in 1892. During the next five years, the best fish weighed respectively 50, 60, 50, 44, 47 lbs by net, and 42, 44, 36, 37, 53 lbs by rod.

Famous stretches

Grantown on Spey has become a very popular centre for visiting sportsmen. It lies some 45 miles (72 km) upstream from the estuary. In 1913 the late Countess of Seafield allowed an angling association to be formed, and gave them access on lease to 7 miles (11 km) of the main river and several more miles of the tributary Dulnain. This created an

opportunity for local and visiting anglers to fish the Spey for very meagre sums. In 1913 a season (eight-month) ticket for a local resident cost just over one pound. In 1989 it cost 35 pounds, but was perhaps even better value in view of inflation. Thus many fishermen can come to Grantown on Spey who enjoy modest sport depending, of course, on the state of the water.

In 1902, Augustus Grimble wrote in his book *The Salmon Rivers of Scotland:* "The Spey angling commences about the top of Lady Seafield's Castle Grant water." He inferred that "between Grantown and Loch Insh there are very few pools or catches." This is not strictly true today, and there are one or two noted beats upstream of Grantown, as at Kinchurdy. Basically, however, the best fishing starts downstream of Grantown, where the Castle Grant water is divided into three beats or sections. These

are owned by Lord Reidhaven, son of the present Earl of Seafield. They can be rented throughout the season, which starts on February 11 and ends on the last day of September.

Immediately downstream of Castle Grant come the Tulchan fishings. After the Countess of Seafield died, these were sold to help pay estate taxes, and are now owned by the executors of Gerald Panchaud, who established a worldwide reputation for the Tulchan Estate. It now offers the visitor a very sophisticated life-style in Tulchan Lodge, and fine fishing on the four stretches, designated A to D. An early booking with the estate is essential.

Much of the Spey is held by regular tenants who take up their option year after year. About the only way of obtaining access in the prime season is to await someone's death, unless you have a friend whose access you can share.

Downstream of Tulchan Lodge, the river widens as it is joined by the tributary Avon at Ballindalloch. Then follows the Pitchroy and Knockando water, among the nicest. Wester Elchies comes next, and is regarded as one of the best on the Spey, although it can have its off days as well.

Some other prime fishing is found at Arndilly and Delfur. The latter has tended to be regarded as the Spey's best beat, but it changed dramatically during the big summer flood of 1970 and has not been such a good spring beat since then. Still, it yields remarkable catches of small summer salmon and grilse.

Nearing the estuary, worthwhile fishing is offered only by the Orton, Brae, Fochabers and Gordon Castle waters. As with all salmon rivers, however, the Spey's potential for sport is dictated by the height and temperature of the water and the time of the season. ❧

The River Dee

Jan Johansson

One can think of many names for a destination as dear as the Dee, and so we hear it also called the Royal or Silver Dee. This famous salmon river

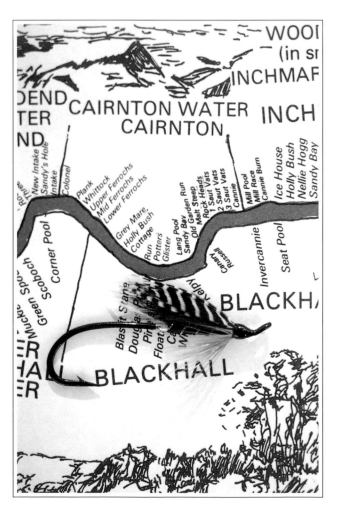

begins its long course in the loftiest mountains of Scotland—the Cairngorms with their peaks of Ben Macdhui and Braeriach, both about 1,200 metres (3,950 feet) high.

The salmon-bearing stretch, from Linn of Dee to the river's mouth at Aberdeen on the east coast, is some 90 kilometres (55 miles) long. Its main tributaries are the Clunie, Muick, Glentana and Feugh. The last-named, full of rapids and waterfalls, is a real spectacle and, when the waterlevel is right, one can even see salmon and trout attempting to run the fall at the Bridge of Feugh.

Under normal conditions, Dee salmon average around 4 kilograms (8.8 pounds), but individuals are caught every year weighing up to 15-16 kg (35 lbs). Previously, quite huge specimens were encountered. The biggest, a salmon of 25 kg (55 lbs), went to Mr J. Gordon in 1886, on the Ardoe Water stretch in the lower part of the river.

The Dee is among the "earliest" rivers in England and, without doubt, among the best rivers in the world for Atlantic salmon fishing. It offers fine sport all spring, from February to May, with a delay that increases as one goes upriver. The upper reaches can be good even into June, though primarily during rainy summers. In June and July, however, the trout fishing can be superb.

A classic flyfishing river

The Dee is a quintessential place for flies, with rewarding stretches that can seldom be matched elsewhere. Like a string of pearls we find the Park,

Chrathes, Banchory, Blackhall, Cairnton, Woodend, Dinnet, Glentana and several others, all of them figuring somehow in the history of salmon fishing.

Many popular types and patterns of flies have been created through fishing in the Dee's pools. Blue Charm is one of A. H. E. Wood's low-water flies, so well-known today. Further familiar salmon flies of the low-water style have their roots in the Dee, such as the Logie, Silver Blue, and Jeannie, which are all covered in George M. Kelson's very readable book *The Salmon Fly* (1895).

Additional Dee flies from the late nineteenth century are often presented as fully dressed flies from the Victorian era: the Gordon and Mar Lodge. A more modern fly from the Dee is the Stoat's Tail, which first saw daylight around 1950 at Park Water.

I would say, however, that flies of Dee Strip Wing type are the most interesting of all the old Dee classics. There are indications in British salmon-fly literature that these flies were introduced before 1850, the best-known being apparently Glentana and Jock O'Dee. Two main characteristics of Dee Strip Wing

Dee flies are characterized by a long, trailing heron hackle and a divided wing.

flies are their long, trailing heron hackle and a wing that is divided, not composed as on other traditional flies.

— 22 —

Many of the legendary salmon flyfishermen once held forth on the Dee, where they sometimes experienced fantastic fishing. Instances of such historic individuals, who have inspired readers of their books and newspaper articles, are George M. Kelson, Fredric Hill, J. Arthur Hutton, Antony Crossley, Eric Taverner, Richard Waddington, and John Ashley Cooper. Perhaps the greatest—Alexander Grant, Percy Laming, A. H. E. Wood, and Ernest Crossfield—never wrote books but, nonetheless, earned reputations as formidable salmon fishermen that have lasted until our day.

The most renowned of them, A. H. E. Wood, made flyfishing history with his floating lines on the Cairnton Water, one of the stretches in the middle part of the Dee. Wood landed no fewer than 3,490 salmon here, most of them with a floating line and small, light flies. His favourite fly through the years became Blue Charm. From Jock Scott's book *Greased Line Fishing for Salmon*, which describes Wood's fishing on the Dee, we learn for example that he caught 158 salmon during the spring of 1927, the Blue Charm taking 99.

Heavy fishing at first

As already noted, the Dee is chiefly known as a river whose fishing is best relatively early in the season. At this time, from February to April, the water is cold and periodically high. Nowadays the choice of

flies is then dominated by tube flies and Waddington flies. Good cold-water patterns in the Dee are Collie Dog, Yellow Dog, Black and Gold, and Dee Royal among others.

Fishing early in the season is heavy and laborious due to the high water, low temperature in the air as well as water, and the occasionally strong winds. Naturally, the longer the season lasts, the more pleasant the fishing becomes, even if the catches do not improve.

In summer, too, the Dee yields quite a lot of salmon, but the required equipment and methods are different. Since the era of A. H. E. Woods—when the Dee salmon were primarily known for being drawn to small, sparsely dressed flies on a floating line—it has been clear that the summer fishing can be terrific. This special kind of salmon flyfishing begins seriously in May, when the temperature rises both on land and in the water. It is a wonderful time on the Dee, when the days are long and nature is bursting with colour. The many bushes of rhododendron and broom that border the Dee are blossoming in May. So why not fish in the Dee even during the warmest part of the year, regardless of whether it demands more from the fisherman?

There is more to the Dee than unforgettable fishing. Visitors are impressed by its rich animal and bird life—not least the plentiful red deer, in the upper valley towards the Cairngorm Mountains. One also has many opportunities for excursions to the local whiskey producers, some of the marvellous castles in the vicinity, or a first-hand experience of nature in the Scottish highlands.

First and foremost, though it is the salmon that provide the leading attraction—at any rate if one is a flyfisherman. ❧

The Gacka

Steen Ulnits

Yugoslavia's river Gacka is a classic that can be traced far back in flyfishing literature. Through the years it has enticed thousands of sportsmen from around the world. The main visitors, of course, have been Germans, Austrians and Italians, who can reach the country in only a few hours of driving. But flyfishermen from distant lands such as America and Scandinavia also wet their flies, now and then, in the Gacka's clear waters. Many have even made it a yearly ritual to fish the river in May, when the big mayflies hatch.

A chalk stream

Most enthusiasts of the Gacka fly into Zagreb, then drive the last 100 kilometres (60 miles) south to the village of Licko Lesce. Along the way lies the lovely national park of Plitvice, with its numerous "hanging" waterfalls—a sight that no fishing tourists in the region should miss.

The Gacka flows across a high plateau, 600-700 metres (2,000-2,300 feet) above sea level. Despite the lofty surroundings, it is a genuine chalk stream. The local mountains are of porous sandstone, which sucks up the precipitation and collects it in underground channels. Here and there the water rises into springs with clean, alkaline water, giving the Gacka a constant pH-value of as much as 7.2. Moreover, the water temperature is 10°C (50°F) year round. So even though the winters are very snowy and cold, down to -30°C (-22°F), the Gacka stays warm and nutritious. Its fish reap an almost explosive productivity. The river emerges from the ground in a small

lake, whose water-power is still used by a primitive sawmill, itself worth a visit. Other sources add to the flow and, surprisingly soon, the Gacka becomes a giant, its lower stretch being 20-25 metres (65-80 feet) wide and up to 6-8 metres (20-26 feet) deep.

Until twenty years ago, the Gacka's 22-km (14-mile) course ended in two natural lakes, where the water flowed back underground and it was possible to catch rainbow trout as heavy as 10.5 kilograms (23 pounds). Yet today these lakes are gone, because the lower river has been dammed up to create a large new lake. Its water is led through a long tunnel down to the Adriatic Sea, where a waterfall 400 metres (1,300 feet) is exploited by a hydroelectric plant.

The state-owned Hotel Gacka commands the upper 17 km (11 miles) of the river. Here only flyfishing is allowed, and it is made interesting by a great variety of fish and food. Eight inspectors—six by day and two by night—make sure the rules are kept. The rest of the river downstream is reserved for members of the local sportfishing association, in the nearby village of Otocac.

Brown trout are grown to a size of 12-15 cm (5-6 inches) and set out at the top of the river. Rainbow trout are grown to about 35 cm (14 inches) and distributed evenly throughout the Gacka's length. These fish develop fast in the rich water. The brown trout—which are completely protected, as they cannot take the hard fishing pressure—become up to 800 grams heavier per year, and the rainbow up to 1.2 kg (2.6 lbs) heavier. As a result, the latter's minimum allowed size has been raised to 45 cm (18 inches), which they reach at an age of four years,

No kill

This fishing takes place in beautiful surroundings. The Gacka flows through a veritable meadow of flowers with yellow, blue and red colours standing out against lush grass. No plant poisons are used here, so the area hums with insect life. Cicadas are heard all day long, falling quiet only if a strong rain-shower passes by.

The water is so clear, even after violent down-pours, that one can easily see fish at a depth of 3-4 metres (10-13 feet). A first-time visitor is stunned by the quantities of fish in the water: several fish may be holding at every metre of depth. The bottom is covered by fine vegetation, with isolated bare patches that leave the fish—or their shadows—plainly visible.

There is deep water right to the shore, making wading impossible since even the longest waders are too short. Long boots are practical when a fish is landed, but normally you can get along well with a short pair. The Gacka is best known for its excellent fishing after large mayfly hatches in May. Then the fish rise to the surface and feast on these delicacies. This is a dry-fly fisherman's dream, although—like most dreams—it is too short.

Thus, on a summer tour of the Gacka, you may be frustrated to see so many fish showing so little interest in flies! The mayfly hatches come to an end, and no fish rise to the surface. But the fish turn their interest to the abundant crustaceans in the river, and become very active near the bottom at depths of 2-4 metres (7-13 feet). A scientific study has revealed

after one year in the river. During this time, they become rather selective, seeing a lot of food and learning to distinguish it from artificial flies. On the other hand, they get used to seeing people and are not especially shy.

that the Gacka may contain up to 20,000 of these tiny creatures per square metre of bottom. So the fish need only open their mouths to be served.

In this situation it is naturally hard to be a fly-fisherman. The fly must be rather small, and be fished deep—a problem technically difficult to solve. But the fish gladly take a minor depth-charge: a lead-weighted weed-fly imitation, tied on a 16-20 hook. To get down to the fish, it should be knotted on the end of a very long, very thin leader. By this means, there is seldom much trouble in hooking the fish. However, bringing them up from the vegetation-rich water is quite another story...

Obviously you cannot put pressure on the fish, but have to tire it out completely before trying to land it. By that time, it is full of lactic acid. Since many of the fish must be released—including all brown trout—this can scarcely be called good sport, even if the fishing itself is exciting.

Once the early summer hatches and big mayfly swarms are over, you therefore face a couple of relatively dull months, with scant activity at the water surface. In August things start to happen again. The mayfly *Beatis rhodani*, familiar in many parts of Europe, begins its autumn hatching. It also occurs on the water in April, and then offers the first true dry-fly fishing of the year.

In September, caddis flies make their serious appearance on the Gacka. The days become chilly and there are far fewer fishermen than in May. But the fish are hungry for these fluttering insects, which conclude the season on this charming river. It's a fine period when you can fish in peace and quiet. ⋇

The Karup stream

Steen Ulnits

For sea-trout fishing among the Danes, what they call the "Karup Å" is the classic of all classics. No other stream in Denmark has been mentioned so often through the years as this one, and often with reference to sea trout in the very heaviest weight class. Hardly any Danish sportfisherman, therefore, is unaware that his country's sea-trout record from 1939 was set here—a shiny migrating fish of 14.4 kilograms (31.7 lbs). For several years the same beautiful catch was also a world record.

Besides being Denmark's best and most stable sea-trout stream, the Karup has excellent flyfishing water. Nobody doubts that this is the stream which has meant most for the development of Danish flyfishing for sea trout.

Swing after swing

The Karup has a considerable length with many pleasant bends and hollows. Certainly no other Danish stream has as many turns in relation to its extent—or, in consequence, as many holding places for both sea and brown trout. Its upper section lies a little to the west of Silkeborg. Then it runs north-north-west towards Skive, where it empties into the muddy, and not especially appealing, Skive Fjord.

In spite of various dams and fish farms along the stream, sea trout can still be caught fairly far up it. To be sure, the upper waters—from the village at Karup station—are primarily known for rather good stocks of red-spotted brook trout. But late in the season there is every cause to keep a sharp eye out. It may very well be a fine sea trout that is tempted by your little trout fly. On the other hand, with a thin 0.20-mm leader you would not have much chance in the plant-rich water!

Apart from the fact that sea trout are found in the upper Karup, the best or at least the most classic stretches are between Vridsted and Resen, downstream of Alheden. In this area lie famous places such as Hagebro, which gave its name to the Hagebro Kro, where many sea-trout fishermen have stayed. Other familiar localities include Höstrup and Koldkur.

Finally one may recall the bends at Wormstrup, the site of the 14.4-kg record trout, taken on a July day in 1939. The renowned hollows of Krogsgaard and Grönbäck are situated along the stretch between Hagebro and Vridsted. Thousands of well-grown sea trout have had to leave their lives on the adjacent green meadows.

The great majority of sea trout are caught on the stretch between Resen and Vridsted—at any rate the fine, shiny migrators. Farther upstream, it is mainly just coloured fish that take the fly, after having lingered upstream for weeks or even months. In addition, the regulated stretch from Vridsted down to a minor tributary, Koholm Å, yields many so-called "Greenlanders" every year. These are small, immature sea trout that swim into the lower parts of the streams during the winter. This phenomenon is known from most of the watercourses that empty into salt water. The colder and saltier the latter is, the greater the number of overwintering sea trout that go upstream.

The Karup is also remarkable for its long-migrating Greenlanders. During cold winters they can be found very far up, until late in the season.

Greenlanders seldom become notably large, and since they eat vigorously in fresh water, they are eager guests when caught on light flyfishing gear.

The fishing

Normally the Karup begins to be fished in June or July. Its sea trout have a solid reputation for being quite difficult to catch, despite the certainty that there are plenty of them—as anyone can see who has visited the stream by late evening or night. Sea trout are, of course, light-shy and do not show themselves much by day. In the dark, however, the water may almost boil with active fish that are enroute upstream, or else simply defending their territories.

Thus only a few sea trout are caught during the daytime, and then only on grey, rainy days when a stiff north-west wind ruffles the water surface. The majority are taken in the afternoon or at night. It follows that, if you are afraid of the dark, you should not entertain much hope of getting sea trout from the Karup; this is best admitted from the outset.

Most of the fish are caught by the local enthusiasts. They know where the fish are holding, and—something which is at least as important by night—they know where to walk, and where not to. The Karup is deep and has swampy banks that, in many places, cannot support an adult fisherman. So when you visit the stream for the first time, you should study it thoroughly by daylight, instead of risking your life along the banks in pitch darkness.

The night fishing is done more or less exclusively with flies—not due to snobbery, but for practical reasons. A fly is undoubtedly the handiest tool, when dark has fallen on the stream. And it is nearly always fished with a double-handed rod, which allows precise presentation even in total darkness.

Using the rod at night

If a single-handed rod is ever seen in action on the Karup, it is virtually certain to be in the service of a travelling visitor. The local people know that only a double-handed rod of 12-13 feet can lay out the fly a few centimetres from the opposite bank, whether by day or dark night. They will also tell you that only a double-handed rod can keep control of a sea trout weighing 5-10 kg (11-22 lbs), or even more, when you have to negotiate the swampy spots along the stream in a nighttime hunt for the hooked fish.

The technique is simple: usually downstream wet-fly fishing. During the day, a fast-sinking line is used

in order to force the fly down to the fish, which are unwilling to rise after it. The opposite method is followed during the evening and night. Then even the biggest sea trout rise gladly for a fly fished with a floating line. But one should keep in mind that Danish sea trout—unlike those in Norway—do not take the fly explosively. They come slowly and surely up to it, just as Atlantic salmon do. Accordingly, you must stay calm and wait to strike until the fish is felt on the rod. Otherwise you risk tearing the fly out of the fish's mouth.

The flies for night fishing ought to be large, of sizes 1/0-1/2, as well as black and bushy. They should be fished somewhat under the water surface or, at some times, even straggling along it. Palmer-hackled flies have many Karup sea trout on their consciences, but nowadays a lot of fishermen use big black muddler flies. These contrast clearly with the night sky and are thus easier for the fish to see.

At all events, it is good to have strong hooks. You may need to apply a lot of power when, at night, a large sea trout sticks its head down into the frequently dense vegetation. For the same reason, a 0.40-mm leader end is suitable. ❧

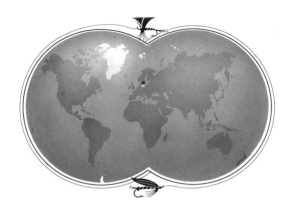

The Mörrum River

Mikael Frödin

A marvel among the world's fishing waters, winding through the lush beech and oak forests of southern Sweden, the Mörrum Stream empties into Pukavik Bay after a final stretch of seven kilometres (4.3 miles) that offers extraordinarily fine angling.

Sportfishing for salmon and sea trout in the Mörrum goes back to the end of the last century. But it was not until 1940 that the fish were demonstrably caught on flies. In May of that year, three Mörrum flyfishermen succeeded in luring some of the stream's heavy sea trout, and in September the first fly-caught salmon was landed, followed a couple of days later by a sea trout weighing no less than 10 kilograms (22 pounds). A treasure of salmon flyfishing was thereby discovered.

Since then, the Mörrum Stream has given up many fly-caught salmon and sea trout of around 20 and 10 kg (44 and 22 lbs) respectively. On May 18, 1979, in Pool 1, the present record salmon was hooked, with an impressive weight of 22.9 kg. This gleaming, fresh-risen male took fifty minutes of dramatic battle to land.

The largest fly-caught sea trout known today was taken in the late 1960s and weighed 12.7 kg (28 lbs). Another well-documented catch is the sea trout that was caught in Pool 3 on September 3, 1947. This magnificent specimen weighed 12.5 kg and was taken on a Chillimps, in the midst of a thunderstorm.

Good spring fishing

Fishing in the Mörrum starts on April 1. During the first two days, the 148 licences are distributed by lottery among thousands of hopeful sportfishermen. For sea trout, the initial days and the following weeks are the high season. The fish caught then are mostly those which have spawned in autumn, and are thus not in top condition, though still fine sportfish. These spring weeks also bring up quite a lot of shiny trout from the sea. They are in fantastic condition—short, thick, glistening fish that offer exciting combat in the frequently fast spring current. At this time of year, the water is high and cold, with plenty of trout eager to bite. The fishing is usually best on the southern stretch, which has numerous excellent flyfishing pools.

Pools 1 and 12 are classics for spring fishing. During the first half of April, flyfishing in Pool 1 is normally so good that everyone who gets a fishing licence can land at least one fish per day. It happens every year that flyfishermen land more than ten fish daily in this pool, but they naturally have to set the majority out again. Pool 12 has its own virtues, provided that the spring flow does not rule out wading. In addition, Pools 9, 10 and 15 are generally enjoyable places to exploit the hunger of sea trout at this time.

The spring season lasts until mid-May, when the water tends to have sunk and its temperature increased towards 12°C (53°F). During the early spring fishing, flies should be fished as deep and slowly as possible. This calls for sinking lines and strong double-handed rods for line class 10-12, as well as reels that hold at least 200 metres of backing. It differs from the fishing later in the season, which is

done almost entirely with floating lines and lighter single- or double-handed rods in class 7-10.

Flies that have proved effective in the Mörrum are, for instance, the Chillimps, General Practitioner, Garry, Mickey Finn, Thunder & Lightning, Black Doctor, Rusty Rat, Akroyd, Red Sandy, and—for early spring—various glittery "Christmas tree" creations. Also for the early fishing, and for autumn fishing, one can use tube flies of size 1.5-2.5" (38-63 mm) and large double or Edmond Drury hooks, whereas for summer fishing the best sizes are 6-10.

Migration upstream

The final weeks of May are the most beautiful and active on the Mörrum Stream. Salmon that come up now are big, shiny and pugnacious. Their weight is usually 8-12 kg (17-27 lbs), but examples of 17-18 kg (38 lbs) are not uncommon. During this period, too,

(Above) *The Chillimps is a classic Mörrum fly, with many large salmon and sea trout on its conscience.*

the real giants of at least 20 kg arrive. Fishing for these earliest salmon should ideally be concentrated to the southern stretch.

Along their journey, the salmon encounter the first currents in Pool 15. Here they gladly pause among the many stones that provide good holding places. The classic Pool 12 is one of the stream's very best fishing spots when the water level is right. Moreover, it is one of the few at which you can do well with long, sweeping overhand casts, to fish the heavy current where the salmon normally hold. Otherwise, salmon fishing in the Mörrum is done with short overhand casts, or—usually due to lack of space—with Spey or underhand casts.

When the salmon reach Pool 11 and pass under

(Left) *This Mörrum salmon weighed 22.9 kg (50.5 lbs)—a record hard to beat.*

the highway bridge, they have reached the stream's first really fast flow. From the neck of Pool 7, the water pours forth between countless stones and, at one point, is divided into narrower flows by small islets. Here a lot of nice fishing spots can be found. An example is the beat under the bridge, where fish often hold. Below the islets in Pool 10, at some inviting deep holes, the salmon frequently show their broad backs in the rapid current.

A couple of hundred metres upstream of the islets, where a big stone block leans out over the water, is one of the classic fishing spots—Smörhålan, the "Butter Hole". Many battles have been played out here, although the hard current and the foaming rapids have often gotten the better of flyfishermen after long salmon rushes and involuntary dousings.

On early mornings and late evenings, the neck of Pool 7 can be quite exciting. Salmon hold for a while in the calmer water and are sometimes fooled by a fly near the surface.

After passing the calm flows of Pools 6 and 7, the fish arrive at the fine little rapid that separates Pools 4 and 5. Here are some lies where the fish hold before continuing under the railway bridge and up into Pool 4. The latter is one of the Mörrum's greatest mysteries: a deep, restful pool with a mirror-smooth surface, it seems to have some secret attraction for the fish, and gathers vast quantities of salmon every year. At the end of the season, its length of about 100 metres (330 feet) may contain up to 800 full-grown fish.

Pools 1 and 4 are definitely the most popular fishing places on the Mörrum. Fish can occasionally be tricked as they sneak past the two islands named Whiskey and Cognac, aiming to pause in the current outside the Laxakvariet (Salmon Aquarium), which

is one of the river's special sights.

At last the fish reach Kungsforsen (King's Rapid), the toughest passage on their migration upstream. Full of white foam—the Virgin Mary is said to have put soap in it—and nearly 300 metres (1,000 feet) long, it is a natural border between the southern and northern stretches.

The northern stretch

Upstream of Kungsbron (King's Bridge), the northern stretch begins with Pool 17. Salmon can rest here after their demanding voyage, so this is a rewarding spot to fish, but the water is deep and it may be difficult to get the fish interested in flies. Once the salmon have passed the quiet-flowing Pool 18, they arrive at Pool 19 ("Grindarna"), which is divided into two channels by an islet.

Farther upstream lie the pools named Borgarholm and Åkroken, where fast beats alternate with deeper water and the fish find many ideal holding places. Next they pick their way through Åkroken's currents and run into another deep, slow part of the stream. But soon it narrows again and the current is compressed in Pool 27. This is apparently preferred by the salmon when the water level is low. At high water, they swim past it and quickly reach the currents downstream of the old salmon traps ("Hönebygget") in Pool 29.

After passing these traps, the fish encounter a stretch that is most reminiscent of an enchanted forest trail. Great trees extend their branches overhead, shading lots of holding places for the salmon. At Pool 31, the stream divides into two furrows—but by walking over a little hanging bridge, you discover a superb fishing spot on the islet's western side, where the water is deep and often hides big fish. The fast current, up to the next hanging bridge, has many fine smooth areas where it can be profitable to wet a fly.

Above the following rapid is Pool 32 ("Rosendalanacken"), a famous and astonishingly beautiful fishing place. The dense birch forest lends unique colour to this classic salmon beat. One is easily taken by surprise when the first big fish arrive after racing up the whole stretch. Dramatic scenes occur every year as hooked salmon leave the pool and throw themselves violently down the rapid. ⁊

Three salmonoids per day are allowed each fisherman. All landed fish must be registered. Fish hooked by mistake have to be carefully released.

Fishing licences should be booked well in advance, normally from January 15 by telephone (0454-50123), or by letter or visit to this address:

Mörrums Fiskeriförvaltning
Kronolaxfisket
S-375 00 Mörrum, Sweden

The Em River

Mikael Frödin

The Em River is the empress of the world's sea-trout waterways. Not only are its sea trout the biggest on the planet, but the fishing for them takes place in stunningly beautiful natural surroundings. The stream winds out of the highland in Sweden's province of Småland, through deep forests and down to the Baltic Sea, where it empties in a powerful rapid. Its fine currents are virtually designed for fly-fishing, and in its holes lurk big fish indeed.

Several world records

Although one can fish on numerous different parts of the Em, it is chiefly the four lowest kilometres (2.5 miles)—undoubtedly among Scandinavia's best salmon and sea-trout waters—that have made the stream famous around the world. This stretch has been in the custody of the Ulvsparre family for more than 200 years. Lieutenant-Colonel Carl Ulvsparre, who introduced sportfishing to the family, was initiated into the art of flyfishing by British railroad workers during the 1870s.

Gustav Ulvsparre, a legendary sportfisherman and fishing conservationist, became custodian of fishing on the Em in 1924. That year he began to keep records of all catches; it shows that 41,338 salmon and sea trout were registered up to 1990. In 1926 the first English sportfishing guests arrived, and in the same journal—which is quite unique today—we read that a Mr. Walter H. Barrett, on 23 August 1926, managed to lure one of the stream's real giants, a male sea trout of no less than 10.5 kilograms (23 pounds). During the following years, many of the

Gustav Ulvsparre with a newly caught sea trout, weighing around 8 kg (18 lbs).

best-known British sportfishermen visited the Em, and enjoyed great success in their "dusters" with the stream's fighting sea trout.

Barrett set a new world record on 7 September 1930, at 8.30 PM in Lawson Pool, with a sea trout of 12.8 kg (28.2 lbs). Eight years later, this was beaten by Calvin Clegg in Barrett Pool, with one of 13.2 kg (29.1 lbs). The latter record held until 1978, when a magnificent male of 13.5 kg (29.8 lbs) was landed on 14 September in Home Pool. A further instance of the Em's incredible champion trout is that Mr. Clegg, on the day he set his world record, tricked two other sea trout weighing 11.2 and 11.6 kg—a series of fish that will probably never be equalled. At present the fishing in Emån is as good as when the English left their mark on it. This is largely thanks to the foresighted fishing management work done by Gustav Ulvsparre for more than half a century. Even

her than quantity, which means that there is a very long waiting list for the maximum of fifteen rods that are allowed during the spring and autumn season.

Shiny spring trout

Fishing in the Em can be done mainly on two distinct stretches, belonging respectively to the Em estate and the Fliseryd Sportfishing Club. The spring and autumn fishing seasons are separated by a ban during the summer, when some salmon come up the river. So it gets a respite until August, and is then ready once more to receive expectant flyfishermen. The spring fishing normally begins around April 1, or as soon as the winter has given way to spring. Water levels are often high and, at times, so high that one can wade out to fish between the centuries-old

The Em has long been a host to salmon-fishing gentlemen such as Anthony Crossley and Walter H. Barrett.

oak trees that border the stream. Due to the cold spring water, sinking lines and large coloured flies are used. On the Em, tube flies are prefered over from the large single-hooked salmon flies that once reigned supreme.

After a few weeks, when the sun has warmed up the water and trees are displaying their first tender shoots, the glistening sea trout begin to run upstream. These short, stocky and warlike acrobats, weighing upwards of 8-9 kg (18-20 lbs), are a true challenge to every flyfisherman, though the spring trout recorded in the Em's catch journal have an average weight of 4.2 kg (9.2 lbs). This period usually continues until May 10. By that time, early summer has come and the majority of sea trout have left the stream for their feeding migrations in the ocean.

now the conservation is handled in an admirable way by the Ulvsparre family, which gives priority to the wild strain of Em River trout. One problem, however, is that the first-class sportfishing attracts all too many enthusiasts to wet their flies in these lovely pools. Still, emphasis is laid upon quality rat-

Biggest in autumn

Commonly the most interesting season is the autumn one, usually beginning on August 20. For it is now that the largest sea trout come up, their average weight being as high as 6 kg (13.2 lbs). These golden-brown fish, with their exquisite patterns, are in a condition that makes the smuggest flyfisherman lift an eyebrow. During the first autumn fishing in August and early September, the water temperature can often be to high. The cautious sea trout are best contacted at dusk with a floating line, a long thin leader and small, discrete flies.

The longer the autumn lasts, the better the sea-trout fishing becomes. In the last weeks of the season, it can again be profitable to try some bigger flies, and to fish them with a slowly sinking line. However, the water temperature and, to some extent, the water flow are decisive. It tends to be at this time that the most gigantic sea trout are landed. Not infrequently, several *Salmo trutta* approaching 10 kg (22 lbs) are caught on the finest days. The season ends around October 10, when the pools are full of trout waiting to spawn.

Unique possibilities

As already mentioned, though, flyfishing in the Em is not confined to the estate stretch. Farther up along the beautiful waterway is the stretch, more than 20 km (12 miles) long, that belongs to the Fliseryd Sportfishing Club. Here one has the opportunities—at the places named Kummlemarströmmen, Klumpekvarnströmmen, Vällingströmmen, Kvillen and Finn Lake—of meeting the shy, yet alluring, Em trout. Fishing in this part of the river begins, as a rule, earlier than at the estate. It can start already on March 1, if the weather permits. The Fliseryd Club

keeps the Em open for visiting fishermen throughout the summer, and usually until mid-October. On this stretch, the best times for fishing are the first weeks in spring and the last weeks in autumn.

The fact that this stretch is also of extreme interest was shown during the spring of 1990 by Roland Maxe, who landed a very fine sea trout of 14.2 kg (31.3 lbs), giving a slight upward push to the world record for fly-caught sea trout. Taken in March, the fish was short and thick, as well as in excellent condition—a real Em trout, in other words. Many different fly patterns have been composed through the years for sea trout in the Em. Among the best-known are Supper Fly, Kräfta (Prawn) Fly, Pilsener, Em-Terror, and Lawson. The latter, my own composition, earned its name one afternoon at Lawson Pool, when I landed two sea trout of 11 and 9.7 kg (24.2 and 21.4 lbs). That day I also caught two salmon weighing 12 and 17.7 kg (26.5 and 39

lbs)—which certainly proves what a dream water the Em River is. ❧

Fishing licences and rooms can be booked through:
Fliseryds Sportfiskeklubb
Box 54
S-38053 Fliseryd, Sweden
Tel.: 0491-92577

The Bod Lake

Johnny Albertsson

West of Östersund, in the mountains of Sweden's northerly province of Jämtland, is an area that has long offered phenomenal opportunities to fish—primarily for large, pugnacious trout. One of these waters is Bodsjön, where English lords began to fish before the turn of the century.

Familiar sportfishing

Bod Lake, like several other waters in the vicinity, is thus historically associated with English flyfishermen and the tradition they brought with them. These sportsmen were not only enthusiastic about flyfishing, but also made sure that the lake was managed as all waters ought to be. In other words, it was taboo to disturb the small fish.

Among the first to fish in Bodsjön was Admiral Edward William Kennedy. The last was another admiral named Stopford, who finally hung up his rod at the age of 80. He then turned the fishing over to a Swedish association (Jämtlands Läns Sportfiskeklubb) with the assurance that the water would be cared for as conscientiously as always.

Already in 1917, however, the initial step was taken towards making Bod Lake a water for sportfishing alone. All fishing rights were leased to Rudolf Hammarström for fifty years. He later wrote Sweden's pioneering handbook of sportfishing, and became editor of a wilderness magazine, *Från Skog och Sjö* ("From Forest and Lake").

Rumours of the fishing in Bodsjön spread quickly, and when Philip Remington England arrived in 1926, he acquired most of the six fishing rights that existed. In addition, he built himself a lovely summer lodge in Bodsjöedet, on the stream between Bod and Tänn Lakes. This edifice still stands, like a sentinel-post at the outlet.

Shallows full of fish

Bod Lake lies in western Jämtland, where the beautiful Indal River has its sources. To begin with, Ånn Lake empties into the Landverk Stream, followed by the Tångböle Stream and leading to Gev Lake. Then comes the Gev Stream, which runs into Bod Lake itself; to the northwest, the Medstugu Stream joins in. The outlet from Bod Lake is into Tänn Lake, with the famous Tänn rapids. Finally come Lake Noren and the lovely Noränge Stream, before descending to the powerful Indal.

Each of these waters can offer wonderful fishing. The region's lakes are inhabited by a well-grown stock of brown trout. Under certain conditions trout migrates up the waterways and provides fantastic flyfishing. What makes the lakes' trout so big is the "storehouse" full of insects they support. The best of these teeming lakes is considered to be Bodsjön. Together with its inlets and outlets, it undeniably makes the sport exciting and diverse. Fairly shallow, averaging about 2 metres (6-7 feet) deep, it contains large flat areas that one has to avoid running the propeller onto the bottom.

There, too, trout and char circulate while they feed on the abundant insect life. Real feasts can occur suddenly when a hatch starts, and then is the time to grab your fly rod. Standing on the shore with binoculars and suddenly noticing such a rise, flyfishermen spring into action like firemen hearing an alarm.

Fast growth

The lake's shallowness naturally creates an ideal situation for flyfishing. Even if a trout takes your nymph on the bottom or in grass, for example, it can rather easily be lured up to the surface by a dry fly—the depth is no greater than that.

Another interesting method, worthwhile during a temporary absence of insects on the surface, resembles the "dapping" that is practised on British lakes. You drift with a boat, provided the wind is neither too strong nor too weak, and cast your nymphs or dry flies in the direction of travel. This is most effective if the wind is slightly rippling the surface, since the fish may otherwise be disturbed by

the drifting boat. One seldom needs to cast very far, but concentration is required so that one has time to hook these quick fish.

From deeper Tänn Lake, past the English fishing lodge, trout ascend to Bod Lake and spend the summer there. During the relatively warm summer months, the trout can get fat on all the insects in the lake's lush vegetation. In autumn, they migrate on up the Gev Stream to spawn.

Trout weighing around 3 kilograms (6-7 pounds) are not unusual in either Bod Lake or its tributaries. The average weight is at least one kilogram, which must be explained by an inherited ability of the fish

to grow well in this environment—and, of course, by the traditionally excellent fish management.

Large flies

Besides the plentiful stock of fat trout, there are char in Lake Bod. These fish stay in the few deep areas, down to about 4 metres (13 feet). At dusk and by night they come up to the surface, and their cautious little rises can be seen everywhere. Char weighing around 1 kg (2.2 lbs) are pretty common, though one cannot judge the fish's weight from the appearance of its rise. On the way home in a boat at evening, their rises can make the water surface look as though a light rain were falling.

The lake teems with mayflies and caddis flies, which thrive in the plant growth. Experience shows that the big trout need to be served large flies in order to tempt them away from their natural food. Another reason why large flies are used almost exclusively here is, to be sure, a lingering taboo against fishing for small trout. This agrees completely with the tradition brought by Englishmen nearly a century ago.

If one looks in the catch journal, it confirms that the big fish are not exactly hungry for tiny, tender flies. The large Streaking Caddis, variants of Muddler Minnows, and Montana nymphs are the choices that regularly occur in the reports. Other popular patterns are Europea 12 and large versions of Ribbed Hare's Ear nymphs.

The Kaitum River

Göran Cederberg

Almost as far up as you can go in Scandinavia, about 150 kilometres (90 miles) north of the Arctic Circle, lies a vast expanse of fells that might seem bitter and barren, were it not for the presence of the Kaitum. To a flyfisherman, this is a paradise of possibilities for catching trout, grayling and char. Here on the roof of the world, in what is widely regarded as the only wilderness left in Europe, run several amazingly beautiful and fish-filled waterways. The legendary Kaitum is one of the very best of them.

For a long time the Kaitum's reputation for fishing has made it a popular goal of travellers. The river is primarily known for its large grayling, but also for good stocks of belligerent trout. The fact that its system includes large Arctic char, as well as very big pike, certainly does not diminish its attractiveness.

Despite the river's remoteness and difficulty of access, sportfisherman from many places have flown to it for many years. The fishing pressure has sometimes been rather great, but there are still plenty of grayling and trout that weigh, respectively, around 1.5 and 2-3 kilograms (3.3 and 5.5 pounds). Every year sees grayling of 2 kg landed, the record being 2.4 kg (5.3 lbs). As for trout, one finds annual specimens of 3-4 kg and a top weight of 4.6 kg (10.1 lbs).

Superb dry-fly fishing

The Kaitum is 100 km (60 miles) long and winds through a lovely valley, which is virtually unaffected by man. Its natural environment reflects the rough climate, with winter for eight or nine months of the year. Hence, too, the fishing season does not begin until midsummer, lasting only until mid-September when the snow and ice spread their mantle across the landscape again.

Normally the fishing is best in the upper parts of the river. The obvious starting-point is Tjuonajokk, a fishing camp at the bottom end of the lower Kaitum Lake—right at the outflow to the Kaitum River. This place, for thousands of years, was a campsite for the reindeer-herding Lapps, an original people of northern Scandinavia. It can offer fishing along a 40-km (25-mile) stretch that is also the river's most scenic one.

The relatively deep valley is surrounded by thick vegetation, mainly of mountain birch. This has promoted rich insect life along the river. Because of the insects, flyfishing is the inevitable means of getting in contact with the fish. Besides the clouds of mosquitoes and gnats, there are stone flies, sedge flies and mayflies in abundance. One thus has a very good opportunity of fascinating and profitable fishing with dry flies. Brown-winged sedge-fly imitations such as Europea 12 and Elk Hair Caddis are suitable, as are large high-floating mayfly imitations. A favourite in the fast currents is Lee Wulff's bushy, hairwinged dry fly—the Royal Wulff.

Days occur, of course, when the fish stay deep, calling for a fast-sinking weighted fly of the pheasant-tail nymph type on the leader. Fish-fry imitations are always effective, especially for trout. Some muddler minnows and dark streamers or bucktails of the Thunder Creek variety can be worth bringing, not least for the big trout in autumn.

Hard to wade

The Kaitum River is fairly broad, with a generally even and calm current. Shallow areas of swift water are seldom more than 1-3 kilometres long, though the speed is significant there. Big stones and deep holes are numerous, and make attractive holding places for both grayling and trout. The fishing is usually best at "normal" water levels and not too high temperatures. Thanks to the large lakes, the temperature is comparatively constant—but the water level can react quickly to rainfall and drought, rising or sinking considerably in just 12 hours.

Grayling are found principally in the fast shallows, while trout prefer the deeper areas with slower water. Really sizeable trout, though, linger in the large deep lakes and are seldom caught with a flyrod.

The fishing is done mainly in the well-populated currents which, on the other hand, are difficult to wade. As a rule, one must go rather far out in order to reach the fish. The bottoms, consisting of great stone blocks, are quite uneven and treacherous, making it essential to have waders and a wading staff at most places.

Among the best-known spots along the Kaitum River are the rapids named Tjirtjam, Taivek and Kukkaksaavos. The first of them lies in the upper part of the water system, about 1.5 hours by boat across the lake from Tjuonajokk. It connects the upper and lower Kaitum Lakes, and is actually at the upper end of the lower lake. This rapid is chiefly reputed for its char fishing, which is sometimes superb. Many grayling and trout can also be found there, of course.

Immediately downstream of Tjuonajokk lies the Taivek rapid, where grayling are the main delight for flyfishermen. Still farther down, on the lowest stretch, lie the Kukkak streams, which offer large trout as well as fine stocks of grayling. It is an undeniable joy to see the fish rise after swarms of insects that periodically circle above the sluggish water mass in the neck of the rapids.

Giants in the lakes

Excellent fishing in the Kaitum is not exclusive to its streams. Its lakes can be extremely rewarding with their grayling, char, large trout and pike. This fishing, however, often requires equipment such as fast-sinking lines, which let the fly reach down to the considerable depths where the fish live. The outlets of small brooks into the lakes are also popular spots, notably for lake flyfishermen who want char. Among the most famous brooks is the Tjuolta, emptying into the lower Kaitum Lake.

Apart from these two lakes, several others with abundant fish exit in the vicinity. The Leffa is renowned for huge pike, yielding specimens as heavy as 18 kilograms (40 pounds), not to mention trout of 4 kg (8.8 lbs). Other lakes are rich in grayling and perch. This wonderful blend of rushing waters and deep, cold mountain lakes is just what makes the region unique for adventurous flyfishermen. ⚜

Tjuonajokk's fishing camp lies about 80 km (50 miles) south-west of Kiruna. It is reached only by helicopter from Kiruna or from Stora Sjöfallet. There are 15 or so cabins, each with 4-6 beds, gas and kitchen equipment for self-service. The camp also has a shop with food, materials for hire, and a telephone. Fresh supplies can be flown in by order. Boats can be rented and, if necessary, fishing guides can help. In the same area are a sauna bath and a fish smokery.

Råstojaure

Gunnar Westrin

*E*urope's finest grayling areas lie in northern Sweden, where good opportunities still exist to catch grayling of 2-3 kilograms (4-7 pounds). As recently as 1966, a grayling with a weight of 3.35 kg (7.4 lbs) and a length of 71 cm (28 inches) was taken in Lake Råstojaure. This is not only a Swedish record, but also a world record for rod-caught grayling. On the same occasion, in fact, about twenty grayling were landed with weights over 2 kg (4.4 lbs).

This remarkable mountain lake, with its very high reproduction of both grayling and Arctic char, is located 100 km (60 miles) north of Kiruna, the northernmost city in Sweden. Råstojaure is on a level plateau with few peaks. To the west, it stretches into Norway, where the highlands begin immediately. The lake is relatively shallow with an average depth of about 5 m (16 ft), an advantage to the fish—and naturally to the fisherman—since the nutrients increase with the water's warmth.

Easy wading

The surroundings of Råstojaure contain both still and flowing waters. Bordering it on the south are Tavvaätno and Kårvejokk; and on the north is Kummaätno, several miles above the main lake of Råstojaure. From the lake run two larger mountain streams, Råstoätno on the east, and the Råsto River on the west. The latter changes its name to the Mås as it approaches the coast, and is one of neighbouring Norway's best salmon rivers. Råstojaure, therefore, is a watershed—in itself a peculiar phenomenon.

Characterizing the local landscape are low mountains and endless heaths, forming an austere environment with much sand and innumerable sandy ridges. Long ago, presumably, it was occupied by a powerful glacial river that brought plenty of stone, gravel, and especially sand. One interesting thing about all this sand is that most of the grayling streams have shiny golden bottoms, which make them easy for flyfishermen to wade on.

The simplest way to reach Råstojaure is by plane from Kiruna. At the lake is a fishing camp which serves as a very good base for the sport, particularly if one is not accustomed to the sometimes temperamental weather. Once at the camp, one finds every facility: it is possible to rent a boat, with or without a motor, and to look for one's own nice spots at a short distance from the camp. One can also, of course, hike away to any of the fishing places in the vicinity, for example across the heath down towards

Råstoätno. There the fishing is often quite good, with almost no high plants along the shores.

The grayling in these Arctic waters prefer to stay in narrow stretches of current. Many big grayling are caught in slow-flowing, slightly deeper streams, where they can calmly eat insects and gorge themselves in anticipation of winter. So the large grayling should always be sought in comparatively narrow, but ideally slow waters—and there is no shortage of them at Råstoätno.

Fishing in the lake itself can be rewarding as well. To a great extent, the voluminous water mass of Råstojaure is reminiscent of an archipelago, with a variety of coves and headlands. The landscape is fragmented, strongly marked by its hills, sandy ridges, tundra, and small to medium-size lakes. Given a bit of luck, grayling—even big specimens—are visible from the land, and with some care one can get them to take a fly. However, it is easier to fish and to move between fishing spots if one has access to a boat, which can be rented at the fishing camp.

Predominant caddis flies

The best time to fish in the Råstojaure area is from July 1 until mid-August. Then the weather is fairly stable, the snow and ice have melted away, and the melt-water from the mountains has drained away. Since the precipitation is mainly on the Norwegian highlands in the west, the area thus has a good position in terms of weather. Moreover, the water level at this time is usually normal. If heavy rain should happen to fall, the water rises instantly in all of the streams around the lake. But this seldom affects the fishing much, and after a day or so the level sinks again. A good spate can actually benefit the fishing.

When you travel to Råstojaure, it is obviously necessary to bring the fishing equipment that may be

required during your stay in the wilderness. Indeed, at least two sets of gear are worth having. The rods should be of AFTM class 6-7, with two reels and two extra spools. Suitable lines are a double-tapered floating line of class 6, and one of class 7, as well as a sink-tip and a sinking line of class 6. If space allows, you are also wise to take a somewhat heavier set, in case the area is hit by hard west winds.

As for the choice of flies, an important point is that caddis flies are the commonest insects in these northern waters. North of the Arctic Circle, caddis flies outnumber mayflies and stone flies by nearly ten to one. Besides imitations of caddis flies, such as Europea 12, your fly box should include caddis pupae in different colours—and small dark flies like Black Gnat, which can imitate reed smuts and mosquitoes. ❧

Flying time from Kiruna is about 30 minutes. Boats and boat motors are rentable at the fishing camp, which also has ten 4-bed cabins and five 2-bed cabins to rent.

For booking and other service, telephone the Kiruna Tourist Bureau (0980-18880) or the Norrbotten Tourist Council (0920-94070).

The Alta

Börre Pettersen

No Norwegian salmon river is as well-known around the world as the Alta. This is naturally because Atlantic salmon do not attain as great an average weight anywhere else. As a result, the Alta has been a magnet for sportfishermen from many countries for decades. Unfortunately, the river has suffered from construction of a power plant—but it will probably continue to uphold its good reputation.

As on numerous other Norwegian salmon rivers, sportfishing was introduced to the Alta by Englishmen. In a book published in London in 1848, Fredric Tolfrey described catches of 65 salmon during two days of fishing, all of them on the fly. Their total weight was 476.5 kilograms (1,050 pounds), and among the patterns recommended were Butcher and Baker.

Fishing only with flies

The Alta lies in Finnmark, the northernmost province of Norway. From its sources near the Finnish border, the river flows north across the expanse of Finnmarksvidda, where it is called the Kautokeino. At Virdnejavre it falls straight down the Alta Valley—and from there to its mouth at Alta, it bears the name of Altaelva. From Virdnejavre, the river runs through a natural environment of unusual beauty, which can hardly be matched in all of Scandinavia. Before the power-plant project, which incited violent protests both inside the country and internationally, this was also the world's finest salmon river. Whether it will be so in the future is

doubtful, but it is certain to remain among the best.

Since 1989, only flyfishing is permissible on the Alta. Until June 24, the fishing is entirely reserved for the local population and is gratuitous. After that date, organized fishing begins. Apart from a short period in July, the fishing licences are divided between local and visiting fishermen, 20% being sold to the latter.

All fishing licences are granted after application. In March, the annual granting of day and week licences for the Alta occurs. Competition for the licences is to be expected, since almost no other river has so few fishermen per kilometre: only about 400 licences are sold for the whole season.

The fishing is divided into five zones: Raipas, Jöraholmen, Vina, Sandia and Sautso. These contain just 76 fishing beats. However, a single licence usually includes several beats. Weekly licences are sold only in Raipas.

Transport to and from the fishing beats is done by boat alone, as there is no possibility of using a car except along the lowest stretches of the river. Boatsmen, or "punters" as they are called, are regarded as professionals on the Alta, because of their knowledge and great experience in order to travel safely on the Alta.

Big salmon

Today no other river offers an opportunity to catch such large salmon on the fly as does the Alta. Nowhere else have so many salmon weighing over 20 kilograms (44 pounds) been taken on flies as here.

The best time for fishing in the Alta is normally from July 8 onward for two weeks. This period is generally rented out to foreign visitors at a very high fee.

One week's fishing at this time—including boat gillies, cabins, food and cooks for six people—cost just over 200,000 Norwegian crowns (about 30,000 U.S. dollars) in 1989. That price covers all zones except Raipas. For Norwegian citizens, though, the cost is about 700 crowns per day—excluding the gillies, who would cost 1,200-1,500 crowns per day. Only day licences are sold in the zones outside Raipas, which has weekly licences.

There are, of course, facilities for overnighting in several zones. Sautogården, Mikkiligården, and Stengelsen lie right beside the river and can be rented by sportfishermen, costing about 1,500 crowns per

day. If several fishermen are involved, the cost is naturally divided between them.

Thus, what makes the Alta expensive is not primarily the fishing, but the travelling (an airplane to the Alta is the only sensible way, for those who are lucky enough to be granted a few fishing days), the boats and their gillies, and the accommodation. Yet to fish for salmon in one of the world's supreme salmon rivers is something that perhaps will be done only once in a lifetime, so it cannot be cheap. Taking a big salmon on a fly rod in almost untouched natural surroundings, with the midnight sun in the northern sky, is such a strong experience that money becomes a trivial matter.

Large flies

We might discuss forever which fishing beats are best in a salmon river, since they vary with the water level and time of season. But if an attempt must be made to name the best beats on the Alta, these should be the Lower and Upper Sierra, the Mikkeliniva, Detsika and Välliniva. At most places, the ideal water level is considered to be between 0 and +1 feet. Some of the beats mentioned, however, become hopeless for fishing if the water level exceeds 2 feet above normal.

Given that only flyfishing is allowed on the Alta, certain fly patterns have gradually emerged that can be called favourites. To be sure, not all of the fishermen use the same patterns. Large, single-hooked flies are traditional on the Alta, and sizes of up to 6/0 are not uncommon. Big tube flies have recently become ever more popular as well. One fly used often by local fishermen is the Sunray Shadow. Among the main classic patterns may be mentioned Black Doctor, Thunder & Lightning, Jock Scott, and Dunkeld; but the Green Highlander, and light-coloured flies, also have their enthusiasts on the Alta. Patterns such as Mar Lodge, Silver Grey, and Silver Doctor can fish very well under special conditions. Even if large flies seem most popular, one should not hesitate to try the same patterns in smaller sizes when tied on double hooks of numbers 2, 4 and 6.

It is not easy to be granted fishing days on the Alta. But if one does get to join the lucky few, an experience awaits one that will not soon be forgotten. Boat tours up the river through wild stretches are, in themselves, powerful enough to move even the hardiest of observers. One just sits in the boat and wonders whether everything is a dream. Then comes the joy of casting a fly across the stream, where the dull thuds of huge leaping salmon blend with the sounds of abundant bird life. When the line tightens, the likelihood of having found a salmon over 15 kilograms (33 pounds) is greater than it would be on any other salmon river in the world. And if this happens in the light of the magnificent midnight sun, a flyfisherman can never be more content. ✖

The Gaula

Börre Pettersen

Everyone agrees that the Gaula belongs to the best salmon rivers in Norway. A few days of fishing here, in the most promising part of the season, can scarcely leave one without any salmon. Fish over 10 kilograms are not uncommon and, later in the season, sea trout may prove to be truly phenomenal fighters.

The Gaula, located in the county of Sör-Tröndelag near Trondheim, runs through scenic surroundings with good connections to the outer world. Parallel to it is a section of the E-6 motorway, as well as the railway between Oslo and Trondheim, while the nearest airport is only an hour's car ride distant. Yet in spite of its central position, the Gaula remains an excellent salmon river.

Large, early salmon

As a place for sportfishing, the Gaula—like many other Norwegian salmon rivers—was discovered by English visitors. Nobody knows just when they began to fish in the Gaula, but it is certain that English sportfishermen stayed on the Rogstad farm at Stören from 1835 onward. Many came to fish for salmon before World War I, but afterward the so-called "Englishmen's period" died out on the Gaula. The flyfishing has continued, of course, and today enthusiasts from near and far can be seen wetting their lines in the fine salmon pools.

The river bears salmon up to Eggaforsen in the Hålt Valley—about 95 kilometres (60 miles) from its mouth—and has a total catchment area of no less than 3,653 square kilometres (1,400 square miles). As

a result, very large amounts of water flow through the Gaula, especially in spring and after heavy rain. On its way to the sea, it also receives water from numerous subsidiary streams. This, in addition, enables great numbers of salmon to go upriver. During recent years, 20-30 tons of salmon have been caught annually by rod in the Gaula.

The fishing season extends from June 1 to the end of August. As a rule, the sea-trout fishing lasts somewhat longer than the salmon fishing, and at this time it is required for all salmon to be released. However, the fishing period can be adjusted from year to year, so there may be changes in the future—and if so, the season will probably be made a little shorter.

Large salmon are in the river already from mid-May onward, but their migration upstream goes on growing throughout June. Small and medium-size salmon are seldom in the river until June turns to July. This is when most of the salmon run that are heading upstream to spawn.

The only natural obstacle which the salmon meet, on their journey up to Eggaforsen, is another rapid named Gaulforsen, about 35 kilometres from the mouth. At high water it can be hard for the salmon to get through this narrow passage—due not to the height but to the strong current. During some seasons, when a late spring sends much cold water, there is not even any point in fishing on the upper stretches before the end of June. Salmon have certainly been known to arrive earlier, yet exceptionally.

A *fine river for the fly*

July and August are the best months upstream of Gaulforsen. Once the salmon have passed there, they need few days to reach the upper end. One can therefore say confidently that the whole river teems with salmon during those two months.

The Gaula meets every expectation from flyfisher- men. One can swing the rod all season long, even though most practitioners do not begin until late June. With a sink-line and large flies, the chances are good of landing a big salmon on the hook earlier. It is then only necessary to adapt to the prevailing con- ditions: until mid-June, the water temperature is sel- dom higher than 8-9°C (46-48°F).

Early in the season, successful flies are those with

patterns dominated by yellow, red and orange. Many flyfishermen use these colours in combination with black bodies. Tube flies are employed more often than traditional flies, but classic patterns such as Red Sandy, Black Goldfinch, Kate and Torrish can be good at the beginning.

The reason why colourful flies are effective in early-season salmon fishing lies in the fact that the Gaula is a conspicuous "humus river". Thus it is frequently brown, and retains this tone during the entire season even if it clears up much later in the summer.

From the end of June onward, extremely colourful flies can be set aside. The time is then ripe for patterns like Thunder & Lightning, Black Doctor and Black Dose. These should be used mainly on cloudy days and during darkness. For days with good weather, such flies as Green Highlander,

Yellow Torrish, Jock Scott and Logie are suitable. In particular, the Green Highlander becomes ever better as the season proceeds. While small flies can fish well in July and August, one should try flies up to hook size 4/0. On the river's rough stretches, large flies are naturally preferable.

Sea-trout fishing in July

Sea trout begin their migration up the Gaula in mid-July. The first to arrive are often the biggest. Farther along in August, the migration intensifies and night fishing with a fly can give very good results. Although sea trout in the Gaula seldom weigh more than 2 kg (4.4 lbs), specimens up to 5-6 kg (12 lbs) occur.

The choice of flies for sea-trout fishing is simple. Most reliable are dark patterns with a touch of red,

tied on double hooks, number 6 or 8. Also well-proven at this sport is the Montana.

The lower parts of the river are best for sea-trout fishing. Since the Gaula has a long salmon-bearing extent, there are good possibilities of obtaining a fishing licence. All kinds of fishing rights are given, but most of the river is accessible with day licences at relatively low cost. However, some stretches are rented out for the whole season and others at exorbitant prices. At Gaulforsen and Frösethölen, for instance, fishermen have been asked to pay several thousand crowns (hundreds of pounds sterling) for a few days. None of these places are better or worse than many other spots on the river, according to fishing statistics. Because of the strong erosion following periods of very high water in the Gaula, a given spot can be good one year and quite ordinary the next.

Definitely bad places for fishing in the Gaula are difficult to identify, as the river has excellent topography in terms of salmon fishing. Still, reservation must be made about the lowest 15-20 kilometres, where quantities of gravel are dug out of the river at the cost of poor fishing results. ❧

Kuusamo

Risto O. Seppänen

Finnish flyfishermen begin to look tense and febrile—indeed, perhaps somewhat devastated—when one utters the magical words Kuusinkijoki, Kitkajoki and Oulankajoki. These waters in the majestic, unspoilt wilderness of northern Finland contain impressively large trout of up to 9-10 kilograms (20 pounds). The trout there reach not only enormous sizes, but also staggering numbers. Big trout by the thousand are caught annually in the streams. And best of all, they let themselves be tempted with flies.

Giant trout waters

Kuusamo lies very near the northern Finnish border with the Soviet Union. In 1989 the Ninth World Championship of Flyfishing was held there. None of the really large trout were caught during this contest, but the ten biggest fish were still 64-74 cm (25-29 inches) long, weighing between 3 and 4.5 kg (6.6-10 lbs)—not exactly small fry.

Visitors to the Kuusamo streams are guaranteed to leave with many memories in their baggage. It is easy to become lyrical, if not religious, after experiencing a fight with a big wild trout on one's fly hook. The chances of an unforgettable take are great indeed at Kuusamo.

A thousand per year

No exact fishing statistics exist here, as Finnish flyfishermen are reluctant to describe their catches. Yet according to estimates, between 300 and 400 large

trout are taken from each of the streams Kuusinkijoki and Kitkajoki, as well as a somewhat smaller number from Oulankajoki. This implies a total of about 1,000 big trout every year.

The average weight is around 2 kg (4.4 lbs), but trout of 3-4 kg are fairly common. Bigger ones of at least 5-6 kg are also caught each season. It is said that the average weight has decreased a little in recent years; on the other hand, extensive stocking of smolt has raised the quantity of fish.

The large trout migrate up from Lake Paanajärvi on the Russian side in order to spawn in these three East Finnish streams. Their migration begins already in early June, with an initial peak between Midsummer and the first week of July. They keep coming up all summer, and another peak occurs late in the season. The fishing can be very good even near the season's end.

Kuusamo's streams are by now famous in the sportfishing world. Only a decade ago, however, relatively few people fished here. The reason was that they had to hike a long way to reach the water. Since a forestry road was built in the late 1970s, visiting sportfishermen have multiplied greatly.

Migrating trout

The fishing season starts on June 1 and lasts until the end of September. But the trout cannot be tempted with flies during their actual migration. Only when they stop to rest or await spawning, in the calmer stretches of the streams, do we have an opportunity. Thus, specific parts of the streams—primarily pools

and the necks of rapids—are what draw attention and attract many visitors. The streams also differ from each other in regard to production of fish: among the three of them, Kuusinkijoki is considered the best, and Oulankajoki the least productive.

As a result, there may be some crowding at the most popular fishing places, and some kind of system is necessary. By local tradition, the fisherman must move rather briskly through the fishable area, so as to make way for others who want to try their fishing luck.

Kuusinkijoki, the southernmost of the streams, is quite varied in character. It has lazy currents in the upper reaches, low pine forests in the middle, and wilder mountains along the lower part. The fishing stretch has a total length of 14 kilometres (8.7 miles) and many rapids. The biggest trout ever caught in Kuusinkijoki weighed something over 8 kg (17.6 lbs).

The region's record trout occur in Kitkajoki—that of 1989 weighed 9.8 kg (21.6 lbs)—but big trout do not arrive up there before about Midsummer. It is mainly on the lower stretch of Kitkajoki that the large trout from Paanajärvi are caught. For the trout migrations are stopped by a waterfall, Jyrävä, although upstream of it there is a stationary local strain of less powerful trout. Whoever tempts the large trout of Kitkajoki should be prepared for a tough hike in real wilderness.

Northernmost of the streams is Oulankajoki, running through a nature reserve where special rule apply. Here the untrammeled environment lends additional interest to the sizeable trout, grayling and whitefish. A contributing attraction is Kutaköngäs, one of the highest waterfalls and a true experience to behold.

Echoes of salmon fishing

The Kuusamo trout, which are not only big but sometimes very big indeed, understandably call for rather heavy equipment. In Kitkajoki, for instance, at several fishing spots it is difficult or impossible to follow a large rushing trout (unless you want to swim). AFTM class 8-9 is a good guideline for choosing gear, and the rod must be able to handle Spey and roll casts because, at many spots, the space for back-casting is limited. The leader should be relatively strong, at least 0.30 mm, while the reel should hold at least 100 metres of backing.

Fishing for Kuusamo trout is very reminiscent of salmon fishing, as the big trout do not feed in the streams. Thus, salmon flies—best simplified variants with hairwings—also work on the trout. The rule is that the flies, except on the sunniest days, should be dark or black, although exceptions do occur. Local fishermen tend to laugh at tourists who visit Kuusamo to catch big trout with dry flies, but it is a fact that numerous fine trout of 4-5 kg (9-11 lbs) have been caught with floating dun hooks.

At the beginning of the season, big trout are taking all day long—primarily on big flies—even if fishing at dusk or by night usually gives optimum results. Later in the season, night fishing with smaller, entirely black flies is most profitable.

Also effective are large streamers, muddlers and spuddlers, especially if they are given a wing that is tied in the Matuka fashion. No matter which type of fly one chooses, it should have ribbing of fluorescent nylon.

At Kuusamo, fishermen talk almost exclusively about the large trout. However, it should be remembered that these streams are among the best grayling waters in Finland. So don't forget to bring light fly-fishing gear as well. If the big trout are missed, as can easily happen to an inexperienced flyfisherman, the grayling—and whitefish in the quieter waters—are considerably easier to make a deal with.

Minimum catch sizes are 35 cm (13.8 in) for trout and 25 cm (9.8 in) for grayling. Information about fishing alternatives is provided by the tourist bureau in Kuusamo: Matkailukeskus Karhuntassu, Torangintaival 2, SF-93600 Kuusamo, Finland. Telephone: +358-(9)-89-221 31.

Laxá

Benny Lindgren

*I*n northeastern Iceland, just south of the Arctic Circle, lava cliffs and sandy shores are slapped by waves from the Arctic Sea. Here lies Laxá, the best-known of Iceland's salmon rivers. It has been visited for a long time by sportfishermen eager to experience the peculiar, almost mystical landscape.

Restricted fishing times

The powers that created Iceland were not overly generous, at least in this region. Its rolling countryside is austere and treeless, naked and wind-whipped. Near the little fishing camp of Husavik, some hours' journey by car northeast from Akureyri, is where Laxá—one of Iceland's hundred salmon rivers —empties into the always shivering ocean. Its name means simply "the river of salmon".

Today it is called "Laxá in Adaldal", referring to the district in question. This is to avoid any misunderstanding, since there are nine other rivers in Iceland with the same name Laxá, a fact which has sometimes confused foreign tourists.

Laxá in Adaldal is a real pearl of dream water—a river that nobody forgets who has ever been there. It descends from a famous lake, Myvatn, and is just 50 kilometres (31 miles) long, about half of the distance being a natural salmon run. In its upper reaches, close to Myvatn, there is also marvellous fishing for stationary trout, which has earned an international reputation during the 1980s. Salmon are thus caught only in the lower parts of the river.

The fishing season here begins on June 10 and lasts until September 9. One fishing day in the best period of the season cost, in 1990, a little over 3,000 crowns (about 50 US dollars) per fisherman. Generally, the salmon fishing in Iceland is most expensive during July, obviously because it is mainly then that the salmon come upriver. The price is only a third as high, though, during the cheapest period at Laxá in Adaldal. Usually at most 20 fishing licences are sold for the river's salmon-bearing stretch, and some people think even this is too many. Yet several fishermen can share the same rod.

The fishing time during each day is also limited, with a morning shift between 7 A.M. and 1 P.M., followed by an evening shift between 4 and 10 P.M. which is changed, after August 20, to between 3 and 9 P.M. No fishing is allowed at other times, when the river has to rest. The fishermen can then be found sitting about their lodges and telling tall tales...

Laxá in Adaldal has a number of tributaries as well. The most important, in terms of salmon fishing, is Myrarkvisl. It bears salmon all the way and is 30 km (19 miles) long. Beats here are limited to three per day, and the fishing season lasts from June 20 until September 20.

High average weights

The summer water flow at Laxá in Adaldal is stable, at about 45 cubic metres per second. This river never suffers from either very high or very low levels. It is quite nutritious and has clear water, which is often unnoticeable since the bottom is made of sharp black lava for long stretches. This stone can also be extremely slippery, requiring caution when you wade.

There is no doubt of the rich yields from Laxá in Adaldal. Icelanders take great care of their salmon, and keep a wealth of statistical data on virtually every river and its fishing.

From 1974 to 1989, the annual average catch of salmon here was about 2,000. In other words, one salmon per rod and day—which may be considered good in relation to most other salmon rivers. The catches during this period, however, varied greatly: there were 3,063 in the best year (1978) and only 1,109 in the worst (1983). On this basis, Laxá in Adaldal is the best salmon river in Iceland from a quantitative viewpoint. Moreover, it has been found that 30% of the salmon are normally caught on the fly.

The average weight of salmon in this river is high, too—actually the highest in Iceland. During the period mentioned, it was up to 5.5 kg (12.1 lbs), a figure that compares well in international terms. According to the Icelandic salmon-fishing journalist Gudni Gudbergsson, the proportion of small salmon—with a year at sea behind them—and large salmon, with at least two years at their places of growth, is 0.43 to 1.

Salmon weighing more than 10 kg (22 lbs), are not so common here, although the river's record, set in the 1940s, is close to 20 kg (44 lbs). During a typical year, about 50 salmon are caught weighing 10-15 kg (22-33 lbs), which means that 3% of the fish reach this size. Yet salmon over 15 kg occur quite seldom.

Favourite local patterns

Many Icelandic salmon rivers are located in barren areas, so they frequently have special fishing lodges where one can eat and sleep. Several of these exist along Laxá in Adaldal, and are usually included in the price of a salmon-fishing tour.

Some of the river's most reliable fishing beats lie downstream of the rapids on the lower stretch. Their names are full of secrets on this saga-rich island: Vesturkvisl, Kistukvisl, Kistuhylur and Breidan, to name only a few. At these places, the salmon are often plentiful. It can easily be seen that, if God was sparing when He made the landscape, He did fill the river with fish—even to the point of crowding.

If you consider wetting your fly in Laxá's green-glowing water, an excellent choice is a single-handed rod between 9 and 10.5 feet long, with a floating line in AFTM class 8-9. A suitable leader thickness is 0.35 mm. For wading, neoprene waders are recommended, since normally both the water and air are cold. A wading staff is not only useful to have, but

essential at many places.

The salmon at Laxá in Adaldal can be tempted with a wide range of flies. Some of the local favourites that have proved successful are Blue Nun, Fox Fly, Draumadis, Laxá Blue, Gullflugan, Nighthawk, Black Sheep, Frances, Hairy Mary, and Dim Blue.

In Iceland, it is perfectly natural to fish for salmon in the hundred rivers they inhabit, and to do so by means of sportfishing. However, the regulations in regard to salmon fishing are strict. As already mentioned, the daily fishing time is only twelve hours, and the number of beats is quite limited on most rivers. This last factor, of course, leads to high costs for sportfishermen. While the average price in 1990 on most rivers was 3,000 crowns, it can be conside-

rably greater on some of them. At Laxá in Kjos, not far northwest of Reykjavik, one had to pay over 10,000 crowns per day in 1990; at Laxá in Asum, during the best period, the daily cost was 17,000 crowns.

Evidently, then, Laxá in Adaldal is by no means the most expensive salmon river in Iceland, despite being one of the very best. 🐟

For information about salmon fishing in Iceland:
Landssamband Veidifelaga
Bolholti 6
105 Reykjavik

Stangaveidifelag Reykjavikur
Haaleitsbraut 68
103 Reykjavik103 Reykjavík

Greenland

Jens Ploug Hansen

The valley is covered in hoar-frost. During the night, snow has powdered the mountains, which gleam white in the dawn. But as the sun climbs, the drifts start to melt and the tent-roofs drip clear, while ice becomes steam in the coffee-pot and the Qingua River rises. Early morning is the best time for flyfishing, when the waters are clear and, against the dark bottoms, one can still see fish—the seagoing char of Greenland.

Fishing in the many rivers of this island is always easy, if you know where the char are. They come upriver in July and August to linger in quiet spots, along current edges, and often below rapids. Every day you can go upstream from the camp and fish pool after pool with red, orange, yellow, black and brown flies—depending on how clear the water is. And the fish take them. There can hardly be any other place in the world where, given the right conditions, flyfishing is as simple as in Greenland. Hundreds of dark shadows are visible in the rivers, and each of them can be lured onto a hook.

Arctic char

Seagoing char exist in much of the North Atlantic. Exemplary areas are Iceland, northern Norway, and on the Canadian side of the Davis Strait—where they can reach sizes of 6-8 kilograms (13-18 pounds). In Greenland they occur all the way from Thule in the north to Cape Farewell in the south, and in numerous rivers along the south coast. This fish is popularly termed the "Greenland salmon", but should not be confused with the true Atlantic

Arctic char in their shiny sea hue (above) and spawning colours (below).

salmon (*Salmo salar*) which goes up the Kapisigdlit River.

Large specimens of seagoing char were once common. We need only go back to the 1960s to find reports of fish weighing 5-8 kg in the rivers at Narssarssuaq in southwest Greenland. Yet, as elsewhere, intensive net-fishing has been conducted during the years at the island's river mouths, resulting in a great decline of the stocks. But protection measures have been undertaken at Narssarssuaq, and the population of seagoing char is now on the way up again. Two rivers at Söndre Strömfjord are also known for their big char, namely the Robinson and the Paradise Valley river. The former is open to everyone, unlike the latter. In the Robinson, char of 3-4 kg (6.6-8.8 lbs) are common every late summer; yet in Paradise Valley, there are fish up to 6 kg. Moreover, it is not generally known that the rivers on the east coast have virgin stocks of char, which still often weigh 3-5 kg. Today, fish of 0.5-1 kg are most numerous on the west coast, though some rivers are entered by specimens of 2-3 kg.

The seagoing char are anadromous, migrating from the sea up into rivers. In June and July they reach the river mouths. Their journey upstream begins during July in southwest Greenland, and during August farther north as at "Sugar Peak", Maniitsoq. Then the fish are shiny and silvery, with many small loose-sitting scales. After a few weeks in the river, they become slightly pink; subsequently a red abdomen appears and the males develop a large jaw hook. Their biting instinct is powerful even while in fresh water, contrasting for example with salmon and sea trout. Thus char, too, are a very popular sportfish on the island.

Flyfishing

In principle Greenland has two kinds of rivers: the big, muddy melt-water ones and the clear ones. In the first kind, fishing is often done with a sinking line, short leader and colourful flies that contain fluorescent material. The flies are fished on the bottom and taken eagerly by any fish that are encountered. The clear rivers flow through lakes where their silt falls to the bottom, making them the most exciting rivers for flyfishermen. These offer quite different

Greenland invites one to fish for char among drifting icebergs.

flyfishing with light, delicate rods of AFTM class 4-6 and small flies of size 10-14. Both nymphs and wet flies can succeed. Dry-fly fishing is unusual, but during periods with rich insect hatches—which mean plagues of mosquitoes and gnats as well—there are lakes and rivers in which the char rise for insects, so that dry-fly fishing may be very rewarding.

In the lakes, char patrol over the transition between shallow and deep waters. Flyfishing is fruitful if your cast can reach out to the edge of the deep water. Yet the weather has to be calm and sunny, allowing the char to show itself at the surface.

Seagoing char cruise along the coasts in June, July and August. The tidal differences are often extreme, and particularly at high tide one can experience dramatic coastal flyfishing on the stones and cliffs, or by wading near the river mouths.

Some visitors also flyfish for stationary char, which occur in many of the waters. But these are not much of a delight, as fish of 30 cm (12 inches) may be up to 15-20 years old...

Remote rivers

Local contacts are often necessary in order to reach the fine char rivers on Greenland. Most natives—and Danes—have boats, which can get to the majority of rivers on the west coast, including really distant ones. Without such help, you have to strike off on your own, either by flying to Söndre Strömfjord, Nuuk (Godthåb) or Narssarssuak, or else by going with some organized travel agency. Tent camps with self-service are popular tours have been arranged to fly the visitor out by helicopter, retrieving him after a few days and proceeding to a new camp, like "fly-out tours" in Alaska.

A fishing licence is obligatory in Greenland and costs about 80 U.S. dollars. You should remember to

take warm clothes, as the temperature can be 4-8°C (39-46°F) even in summer. Mosquitoes and gnats are a problem at times, though they seldom lessen one's fishing fever. For on Greenland, you still have the chance to engage in some of the last great adventures in flyfishing. That is, if you want to lay out a fly at every cast over hundreds of schools of seagoing char, which hold as densely as the sockeye or coho salmon in an Alaskan river. ❧

For more details about fishing in Greenland, contact:
Diana Fiskereiser
Skårupöre Strandvej 54
DK-58881 Skårup, Denmark
Tel.: 00945-62-231110

One then lives in Nuuk and flies daily to new rivers. Tent trips cover the area around Narssak and Narssarssuaq. Flying tours go to the Godthåb Fjord, where one fishes for example in Qoorqqut Lake, the rivers Natsilik, Kobberfjord, Kanasut, and the Kapisigdlit—the only river where Atlantic salmon run.

The Eagle River

Steen Ulnits

Salmon and Labrador are inseparable from each other. Labrador is well known for its many rivers abounding in salmon, particularly smaller ones weighing up to a couple of kilograms, which give this region the same advantages as Iceland.

Whoever has fished for salmon elsewhere in the world feels surprised when first standing on the banks of the Eagle, which is among the most reputable salmon rivers in Labrador. Along the lowest stretch near the sea, where most of the salmon are caught, the water is wide and deep. Fishing is done there mostly from canoes, anchored above the large pools. Wading can be done only in certain places, and at low water levels.

Small flies

But the Eagle is a fairly extensive waterway and changes its character farther up. Near Park Lake, for instance, it is least like a stream. Looking at the whole of it from on high—in a helicopter or a seaplane—one sees, instead, numerous small lakes that resemble pearls on a string. These still waters are connected by relatively short stretches of stream, and it is here that the salmon lie, not in the lakes which they rapidly traverse.

Thus, the holding places may be widely separated in the Upper Eagle River: so widely that you need a canoe or, better yet, a helicopter when moving from pool to pool. This also means that a first-time visitor can find it rather hard to locate the salmon's holding places at all—unless the fish show themselves above the surface by leaping high.

The greatest fishing pressure occurs, naturally enough, on the Lower Eagle, where the vast majority of salmon are caught. Close to the coast, the fish shine like silver and are eager to take, becoming brilliant fighters with fire in their tails. When they reach farthest up the river, they are more or less coloured, but one can still make contact with them by using small flies on a floating line. Anything else than a floating line is hardly usable in the Eagle, whether far upstream or right down at the sea.

Days on the Upper Eagle

The fishing season on the Eagle, as well as throughout Labrador, is from July until the middle of September. It is often possible to travel most of the way along the river by canoe, although very low water levels may force one to pull the canoe by hand through the worst rapids. On the great quiet stretches between rapids, a motor is best relied upon to save time and energy. It can take a day or more to reach the intended campsite, but along the way one can take the opportunity to fish carefully through interesting pools. In regard to campsites, a good idea is to bring some sort of fire-stove, which prevents freezing and helps to dry clothes. With the base camp as a starting point, one can then shift between the pools that lie within reasonable boating distance.

It is sometimes a bit difficult to find the fish and their holding places. A little patience may be needed before acquiring an eye for this river's special character. But then you can start catching fish—and enough to get by on, even if not very many.

Although mainly small salmon of 2-3 kilograms (5 pounds) may be landed, "real" salmon of 5-7 kg (11-15 lbs) occasionally also appear from the depths to take small flies.

The salmon in the Eagle are not conspicuously large—they seldom exceed 10 kg (22 lbs)—so it is not their weight that determines the equipment. What does is the wind, which tends to blow constantly up and down along the river, in spite of the dense forest. Even well-executed double hauls with a WF-8 line will commonly end as a tangled heap behind the caster, however adept he is. The harsh weather conditions are definitely the governing factor in Labrador.

The lightest gear required for this fishing is AFTM class 8. Yet many veterans prefer equipment all the way up to class 10, because of the wind. Ordinary salmon flies of sizes 2-8 will catch fish, but large weighted muddlers that fish deep are also effective in the Eagle. A special favourite is the yellow-

green Cosseboom, an American hairwinged answer to the classic Green Highlander. Its colours evidently are appreciated by the fish in these tea-toned waters. Moreover, the same tea colour recurs in most of Labrador's flowing and still waters. As in other places, though, it is the presentation of the fly that is entirely decisive, the actual pattern usually being a secondary matter.

Blowing and raining

The fact that fishing in the Eagle River can be extremely good is shown by the following experience, which I had some years ago. It was late one afternoon, clearing up in the west after a couple of days' continual wind and downpour, to make a memorably beautiful evening.

With less than two metres of line outside my top

eye, I caught two lively young salmon almost immediately. Both took to the air three or four times before being landed and released. This was amazing, as I had hardly begun to fish, with only a few trial casts in the shallows.

Next I waded farther into the current, toward a stone where I had previously caught several salmon. My Cosseboom descended with a plop in front of the stone, swung out slightly into the stream, and suddenly—it was taken by a fine fish.

However, the culprit this time was not a salmon, but a 1.5-kg (3.3-lb) brook trout. It quickly exited to the main stream and turned broadside. Once I had landed it, I laid out the fly again before my stone, and the same thing happened. Such was the case with the following five casts as well. Since my catch was now up to seven nice trout of 1-2 kg (2-4 lbs), with no misses, I took a wild chance at ten trout in ten casts. Tragically, I didn't get the tenth trout until the twelfth cast...

Now I was nearly intoxicated. Fish after fish fell for the fly, in exactly the same square metre at the same stone. They must have gathered there to await the imminent spawning period. It therefore felt unreal to wade as far as the outermost stone, lay a cast across the current, mend the line—and hook a big salmon.

A second later, this fish leapt from the water in a high arc that sent cascades of water through the red sunset. For a moment we looked each other in the eye, and then the metre-long creature rushed downstream.

After two more rushes, it was calm enough that I could begin the long, hard return to land. Reluctantly the salmon followed me into a wide backwater, where I carefully beached it and beheld a female of 7 kilograms, shimmering like silver. Her belly was full of roe, so I handled her gently before releasing her back into the river. ⚜

The Minipi

Steen Ulnits

Salmon in the Canadian province of Labrador are abundant, but seldom very large. They usually weigh well under 10 kilograms (22 pounds), and small ones are predominant. By contrast, in the north of this region, one can catch what is perhaps the world's biggest Arctic char—enormous fighters of 5 to 10 kg (11-22 lbs)!

Yet the fame of Labrador among the world's flyfishermen rests on its squaretail. This exotic fish, whose natural stocks exist only in the northeastern United States and Canada, reaches maximum weight in the Labrador wilderness, and weights up to 3 kg (6.6 lbs) are not uncommon in some waters.

At Goose Bay is the mouth of the great Churchill River, which drains a good deal of Labrador. Far up at Churchill Falls, we find the giant Smallwood Reservoir, a hydroelectric dam with several flooded lakes of varying extent. This dam delivers power to eastern Canada and is important for the country's economy. Sportfishermen are more interested in the fact that these artificial lakes provide a home for big "namaycush", the American lake trout.

Large flies like this deer-hair mouse are the secret of catching Minipi's big squaretails.

Sizeable squaretail

One of the tributaries to the turbid Churchill River is the clear, but tea-coloured, Minipi. Inhabited by the world's biggest squaretail, it belongs to a complex water system that includes a chain of lakes connected by short streams. There are no streams, however, leading from the long, windy Lake Minipi.

The larger lakes in the Minipi system are deep and contain big trout, while the lesser lakes are rather shallow and, as a result, highly productive. These are characterized by rich insect life, especially mayflies such as the huge *Hexagenia*, as well as caddis flies. It is in the little lakes that the Minipi's squaretail grow to record sizes.

In general, squaretail live only a few years. They stay in confined waters with scant nutrition, and thus tend to remain small—rarely exceeding 1 kg (2.2 lbs), and usually being even tinier than that. But in Minipi's water, they live comparatively long, up to ten years; and thanks to the ample supply of food, they grow explosively. The rule of thumb is that their weight increases by one pound (about 450

grams) for every year in the lakes. The largest go over 4 kg (8.8 lbs), and a considerable number are in the 2-3 kg (4.4-6.6 lbs) class.

The shallow lakes are warmed up rapidly by the sun, reaching temperatures of more than 15°C (59°F). This is pretty hot, given that Labrador is rather far north. Moreover, there is a big stock of pike that grow very well. The pike live, of course, on squaretail, which means that the latter have to grow fast if they want to avoid being eaten up.

A flyfishing paradise

The streams connecting the small lakes are rarely more than a few hundred metres long, so most of the fishing is done in the lakes themselves. This takes place from boats—either slender canoes, which are ideal for sneaking up on rising fish, or else larger vessels that can also sail the big lakes easily. Fishing with waders is possible only on occasion, as the bottoms are usually too soft and the stones too slippery, or the shores are too heavily overgrown.

It was Lee Wulff who, in his day, discovered the fantastic fishing in the Minipi system. Later this region was explored by the American expert Ray Cooper, who built the first proper fishing camp—a predecessor of the few lodges that exist there today. In Labrador, the law says that a foreigner can fish only in company with a local guide, never alone.

Almost all the fishing is done on flies, and this is a

perfect Eden for dry-fly fishing. From the season's start in June until the middle of July, mayflies and caddis flies hatch in vast quantities all over the lakes. There are so many of them that even fish of 3-4 kg (6-9 lbs) eagerly rise to the surface. After mid-July, these hatches stop—but during quiet evenings one can still experience amazingly fine fishing with dry flies. This is when the gigantic *Hexagenia* mayflies swarm, and if you are lucky with the weather (which can be a problem at such high latitudes) it may yield the best dry-fly fishing of your life. Catches of 3 kg (6-7 lbs) on dry flies are routine throughout the period.

The fish are seldom very selective, and most are taken on big bushy dry flies of sizes 6-12. It is hardly surprising that Wulff flies are among the local favourites. An ample collection of Grey and White Wulffs can do nearly all the work. And when the fish are not rising, you can put a muddler on your leader instead. Normally only floating lines are used in the small lakes, and this naturally makes the fishing more enjoyable.

During some years, the forests of Labrador become overcrowded with mice. They push out into greener pastures, just like lemmings—and every night, many of them jump in the water to cross a river or lake. A lot drown on the way; others are eaten. At night they can be seen swimming in the moonlight, or the aurora which may flash over the sky in the wee hours. By morning, the bodies of dead mice are found lying and floating everywhere.

The pike are glad to gobble these creatures, as is well known. But so are the big squaretail, a fact that often escapes us. Consequently, the largest squaretail are best taken with a floating deer-hair mouse when such "mouse hatches" occur. It is thus important to have mouse flies in your box, besides the more common types of dry flies.

Catch and release

It was realized already by Lee Wulff that the big squaretail in this water system are a weak stock. The species was, as it still is, relatively easy to catch—and many a flying machine was filled with the bounty. Wulff's experiences made him a keen supporter of "catch and release" fishing, which is simply a necessity here.

Most of the region's fishing lodges allow their guests to take only one trophy fish home—for preservation, as is common in many parts of North America. The rest have to be set out again. From time to time, some small fish are caught for dinner, but these are very few. On the whole, this policy has enabled the large squaretail in Minipi to remain as plentiful now as they once were. At regular intervals, the area also produces world records. 🎣

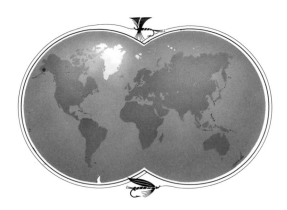

Lake Iliamna

Steen Ulnits

Alaska is rightly renowned for its fine sportfishing for salmon, trout and grayling. Few other places in the world have such a great range of species, and almost nowhere else is the fishing so well organized. Here you can find lodges, outfitters and everything else that satisfies your desires when fishing.

A visiting flyfisherman's interest usually focuses on the large inland Lake Iliamna, in south central Alaska. It offers a rare experience of varied fishing for many species, and a unique size of rainbow trout. Several waters have received trophy status and particular fishing regulations, naturally for the purpose of keeping the fishing as good in future as it is today.

Pacific salmon

If you are looking only for chinook salmon in the record class, you should concentrate on the Kenai Peninsula. For record-size coho salmon, a better place is, for example, Kodiak Island. But when it comes to areas with all five species of Pacific salmon represented, nothing can beat the surroundings of Lake Iliamna.

Diversity is the hallmark of this lake. Since most of the area's waterways are crystal-clear and virtually created for flyfishing, it is no wonder that enthusiasts flock here during the short summer months. One can "sight-fish" for gigantic chinook salmon, or cast roe flies for roe-eating rainbow trout, Arctic char or grayling. And here one can see grayling half a yard long rising to small dry flies. During August,

one may stand in pods of fresh-risen coho that attack every streamer or bucktail. Not to mention fishing for steel-grey and red sockeye salmon by the hundreds of thousands, which come up from Bristol Bay in July!

In late June and early July, the big chinook arrive from the Pacific. They attract a very special kind of flyfisherman, who fights these giants with heavy equipment in class 10, plenty of backing, and strong leader tippets. The fish average over 22 pounds (10 kilograms) and have enormous reserves of energy after vacationing at sea. Such an encounter often ends with an empty reel, a snapped leader, or even a broken rod.

Other salmon fishermen prefer somewhat lighter gear and wait until July, when large schools of sockeye appear. This red salmon, once considered almost impossible to catch in a sporting manner, is the ideal

prey for equipment in class 7-8. Steel-grey and fresh-risen, it is pound for pound the strongest and wildest of all Pacific salmon.

Many visitors to Lake Iliamna wait till August, however, when the first coho salmon show up in the river. These are widely regarded as the best sportfish among salmon, since it rushes far and leaps high. At the same time, it is definitely the most beautiful member of the salmon family. The two remaining Pacific salmon species—humpback and chum—are less appreciated by flyfishermen, because they go out of condition soon after arriving.

Roe and roe flies

Pacific salmon provide not only fantastic fishing, but also indirectly a distinctive kind of fishing: with roe flies for rainbow, char and grayling. All the salmonoids around Lake Iliamna depend heavily on the large salmon rise. For these smaller fish can feast on the roe which is caught by the current and pulled down into the water.

When the salmon are spawning most intensely, roe becomes the main diet of the rainbow, char and grayling. It is obvious that, to play the same game, you must put a roe fly on your leader—a little Glo Bug in fluorescent colors, or a smaller Iliamna Pinkie

with chenille body. Roe flies are fished just like weighted nymphs, with a floating line and a long leader. The fly itself can be weighted, but then it will not follow the current as natural roe does. So a better method is to weight the leader with a shot or two.

The large rainbow trout are primarily what have spread Lake Iliamna's reputation around the flyfishing world. Several of the biggest fresh-water rainbow are caught here regularly—fish that have benefitted thoroughly from a nourishing stay in Iliamna or some of the area's other extensive lakes. They can be fished for all summer, but the really big ones are usually caught only at the beginning and end of the season.

On Iliamna, the season starts in June, chiefly with fishing for large rainbow which are heading downstream—out in the lakes—after the previous year's spawning. Before leaving the streams, they are best caught on dry flies; and then they often weigh 2-3 kg (4-6 lbs), even if they are still a bit thin and in bad condition.

Yet the autumn fishing in September and October is completely different. The many summer tourists are gone, and you see only a handful of hardly flyfishermen with record-size rainbow on their minds. For it is at this time that the year's whoppers are caught in Iliamna: silvery, well-fed giants approaching 10 kg (22 lbs). Not on dry flies, though, but on large weighted flies that are fished with fast-sinking lines, as the weather is cold in September and, in October, there can be storms as well as snow and frost.

Drifting downstream

While fish can be found everywhere around Lake Iliamna, some places are naturally better than others. One historic choice is the white-foaming Newhalen River, which flows from Lake Clark and empties into Iliamna on the way to the sea. The Newhalen is renowned both for its colossal run of sockeye salmon in July, and a much smaller run of significantly bigger rainbow in September and October.

More openness, and at least as big rainbow, occur

The Great Nushagak is formed by the Little Nushagak and the Mulchatna River. The latter's tributaries are particularly popular with flyfishermen, whose ears are pleased by names like the Chilikadrotna, Koktuli and Stuyahok. If your interest turns to big, shimmering, newly risen chinook salmon, it can be well worth paying a visit in July to the Kvichak River—flowing out of Lake Iliamna—and to the Alaagnak which leaves another big lake nearby. ❧

for example on the Lower Talerik Creek, Gibraltar Lake and Copper River. Smaller rainbows, Dolly Varden and grayling of 1-2 kg (2-4 lbs) exist in most of the streams. But the best flyfishing is in the smaller waterways, where one can often see the fish.

An enjoyable means of experiencing the fishing and natural surroundings in this region is "rafting". This means drifting downstream, equipment and all, in big rubber boats and camping wherever one wants. It brings one into direct contact with the fish as well as the environment in Alaska's fantastic wilderness. The Great Nushagak River, is a fine goal for this adventure.

The Skeena

Steen Ulnits

Along the west coast of North America is a number of very large river systems, two of which are important to flyfishermen. The southern one is the great Columbia River—and the northern one is the Skeena, in Canada's province of British Columbia. The Skeena is best known for its wild Pacific salmon and steelhead.

Along the Skeena, habitation is still thin and there is much less industry than farther south. This water system has, until now, been spared the presence of hydroelectric plants with their big reservoirs that separate the fish from spawning places upstream. Consequently, the Skeena's swimmers are genuine creatures of nature, born and raised in its cold, unpolluted currents.

With its many tributaries, the Skeena is among the most prolific of the Pacific salmon rivers. All five American species are represented here: from the mighty chinook and the smaller chum, humpback and sockeye, to the little but leaping coho. Their journeys upstream are distributed evenly throughout the summer. Chinook come up already in June, followed by the chum, humpback and sockeye. Last to arrive—in August and September—is the coho, whose silvery and frisky ways make it the sportfisherman's favourite.

Big steelhead

The Skeena's mainstream is broad, with water coloured milky by suspended clay particles, so that it resembles the other large water systems of the west coast. Only towards autumn, when the level is lowest, can one begin to flyfish in the mainstream itself, as the fish can hardly see the fly until then. After sudden rain, though, the water may once again look like a cup of thick chocolate.

For this reason, the smaller tributaries become more interesting to us. Their size allows one to wade and cover the best lies with a fly. In addition, the water is usually clear and perfect for a floating or sinking line—whichever the water temperature indicates.

Steelhead, the seagoing rainbow trout, are what primarily attract flyfishermen from all over the world to the Skeena. Almost nowhere else can one still catch such big specimens, and weights of 10 kilograms (22 pounds) are nothing out of the ordinary. These fish are extremely abundant because the Skeena is genetically adapted to late first-time spawning. They just stay put in the Pacific's ample food-stores, enjoying long voyages in the best salmon tra-

dition, before their initial maturity leads them back to spawn. It is this priceless peculiarity that provides the Skeena with a unique wealth of steelhead.

Formerly, the Skeena was famous for its early rise of so-called "summer fish", the shiny steelhead that came up already in July. But this stock has sharply declined, due to the intensive salmon fishing in the sea near the river mouths. Despite a ban on catching or selling those steelhead, thousands of them die as a by-catch of the commercial salmon fishing in summer.

As a result, flyfishing for steelhead now occurs later in the season than it once did. The best and most reliable fishing can be found in the Skeena's smaller tributaries during September and October. Most of the fish, however, are more or less coloured, and the water as a rule is so cold that you need a sinking line and big flies in screaming colours to awaken the fish's attention.

Luck with the weather, and water temperatures around 10°C (50°F), enables you to experience how these huge fighters snap at small flies in, or slightly under, the surface on a floating line. This is dream fishing for any fly enthusiast. You must, on the other hand, expect to need a sinking line, exactly as if it were meant for salmon.

Renowned rivers

While the quest for steelhead is unlikely to be disappointed in several of the Skeena's tributaries, some of them are well above the average. Starting farthest down near the Pacific, there is the Bulkley River, which has gained a reputation for exciting sport with floating flies that can straggle in the surface. Often the fish rise more than once to these flies before deciding to take. Best known is the Bulkley Mouse, a deer-hair pattern that has chalked up a lot of trophies to its credit.

Upstream are the Babine and Kispiox, two rivers which for many years have yielded countless record-size fish, including world records. The fishing here is usually late and cold, with heavy sinking lines and large flies—a hardy sport that has many devoted followers in both Canada and the United States.

Highest up, we find (though it's not easy to reach!) the Sustut River, whose name has spread seriously only in recent years. Apart from its many big steelhead, nearly a third of the chinook salmon in the Skeena water system come up this river, making the fishing a riotous business in July and August. Since it is far from the sea—almost 250 miles (400 kilometres)—the fish are all coloured at that time.

The seagoing rainbow trout is recognized for

power and pugnacity when taking a fly. Yet after a long, difficult swim up a water system, the fish are tired out by having to force the strong currents, or weakened by staying in fresh water without food. So they frequently offer only a few minutes' struggle and then give up. At such a spot, you should not be surprised if a hooked steelhead follows obediently in to your rod end. It is already half-beaten by nature, and why it even takes the fly is a mystery.

Colourful flies are needed to attract the silvery steelhead in the murky Steena

Regulations

Steelhead fishing in the Skeena and its tributaries will probably soon become a "no kill" sport, meaning that every catch must be released. For the present, however, there are only limitations on the number of fish that an individual can remove every year. Sportfisherman are also encouraged to use barbless single hooks. The days when one could luxuriously execute valuable wild fish are, it seems, gone forever.

Fishing in British Columbia has long been relatively cost-free for both natives and foreigners. A very small fee could acquire a fishing licence for the whole province. But the authorities have proposed restrictions on how many foreign fishermen can enjoy the most popular steelhead rivers, including the above-mentioned Skeena tributaries. These rules mean that there will be less crowding on the best waters. At the same time, they create new jobs for local guides, who will be given a yearly number of rod days. This is a parallel to eastern Canada, where foreigners can fish only in the company of a paid local guide. ❧

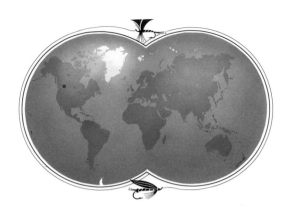

The Bow River

Erwin A. Bauer

I am not likely to forget a raw, bone-chilling afternoon several years ago in southern Alberta. Early in the morning we had debated whether to go fishing at all, because a major storm front that promised snow was approaching from British Columbia. But flyfishermen do not always act sensibly, especially when the season is drawing to an end and few days remain on the river. So I stood shivering, thigh-deep in a cold current, casting at random with an eye on the heavens. No trout were rising anywhere in sight.

My mind wandered and I noticed large skeins of geese and ducks flocking southward. All around the landscape was depressingly flat. A cold wind blew from behind me, downstream, raising small whitecaps. A line of dense gray clouds was continuing to build in the northwest; soon we would have to leave the water.

Then my Black Woolly Bugger streamer fly snagged on vegetation, and I raised my fly-rod tip sharply to release it. But the "vegetation" was alive, and began to swim slowly upstream. That is how I happened to hook my largest-ever brown trout on fly tackle. About fifteen minutes later, the weather forgotten, at a considerable distance from where I had started, I slipped a net under the splendid fat fish. I will never know exactly what it weighed, as I clipped the leader and watched it swim away. But I am convinced that my estimate of about seven pounds (3.2 kilograms) is conservative. As far as I know, that trout is still swimming free in the Bow River, perhaps a pound heavier and maybe even with a Woolly Bugger deep in its lower jaw.

Unique water

The Bow River of southwestern Canada stands out among great trout waters for a number of reasons. It begins in Banff, one of Canada's exquisite national parks in the northern Rocky Mountains. There, and for most of the 60 miles (100 kilometres) southward to Calgary, a load of fine glacial silt colors the Bow a powdery blue. Only a few whitefish live in this stretch of water. But suddenly, almost miraculously, the character of the river changes at Calgary.

Elsewhere around the world, the effluent pollution of large cities often destroys the rivers that pass through them. But the nutrients that survive the Calgary (population 700,000) water-treatment system (or the lack of it, according to some citizens) enriches the next 50 miles or so of river almost beyond an angler's imagination. As a result, today the Bow is vastly different from what it was a century ago. Now it is lush with aquatic vegetation, contains a huge and varied insect population, and has trout that are larger than average. In other words, it is Dream Water.

Another unique feature of the Bow is its width, much greater—for long distances—than that of a football field. From Calgary for about 30 miles (50 km) to the Wyndham-Carseland Provincial Park, flowing eastward, it resembles a super European chalk stream, but with a slightly faster current. The flat countryside all around is part of the North American breadbasket, planted in wheat. Here and there, cottonwood trees and low rocky cliffs form the river's edge. Altogether it is not the most inspir-

ing scenery that one usually associates with trout rivers.

Brown and rainbow trout

Until the last 10-15 years, the Bow remained the well-kept secret of a few Alberta trout fishermen. Only recently has it been discovered that excellent sport is possible beginning at the southern outskirts of Calgary. In 1988 a local newspaper reported that a 12-year-old boy had caught an 8-lb (3.6-kg) trout almost beneath the busy four-lane Deerfoot Trail (Route 2) within the southern city limits.

About 30% of the Bow River trout are browns, the rest being rainbows. Their average weight is an astounding 1.5-2 lbs (0.7-0.9 kg), and specimens up to 4-5 lbs (2 kg) are fairly common. Both species enjoy rapid growth rates on the ample insect diet. This river may be any outdoorsman's best bet to capture a trophy trout in North America on a summer day.

The combination of hot weather, sudden savage thunderstorms, and the heaviest weed growth make August the poorest fishing month. But even so, the action is far from slow. The best times are early summer and the golden days of September.

Most active guides on the Bow rate July as the best month for dry-fly fishing. Many also note that October is a prime time for anyone who does not mind the frosty mornings and frequently windy afternoons.

Small flies

For the entire 30 miles below Calgary, the Bow travels through private lands. This not only makes public entry difficult, but also means that—to fish by watercraft—one must launch a drift boat, infla-

table raft, or shallow-draft johnboat only at the limited access sites. Alberta law permits free use of the river: floating, anchoring and wading, going ashore (even camping) on river islands. Yet trespassing on lands that border the river without permission is illegal. The result, of course, is that numerous guides and outfitters have become established in the Calgary area to serve visiting flyfishermen.

In his excellent *Western Fly Fishing Guide* book, the expert angler and aquatic entomologist Dave Hughes writes that Pale Morning Duns in size 16 match the primary hatches of late June through July. Very tiny flies, such as size 20-22 Tricos, are suitable for August and September insect hatches. Small Blue Wing Olives work well through September and October. So does an Adams fly in sizes 14-18.

At intervals all summer long, evening caddis flies hatch in clouds. Then many of the hopper imitations—such as a Joe's Hopper, Goofus Bug, or Elk Hair Caddis—will be effective. Large trout especially feed on the abundant leeches, for which the Olive Leech or Black Woolly Bugger are superb choices of flies. A Fanwing Coachman is always a good pattern to try.

The continued health of the Bow River is somewhat guaranteed by the fact that few of the trout are ever removed from the river, even though the limit is two small fish per day. Fish longer than 16 inches (40 cm) must be released. But that is not hardship, as Bow trout are not really palatable anyway.

Air service to Calgary is uncomplicated from anywhere in the world. Accommodations of every category, top to low-budget motels and hotels, exist in Calgary and the suburbs. The fine campground at Wyndham-Carseland Provincial Park may be crowded or full during midsummer. ❧

The Deschutes river

Dave Hughes

The Cascade Range is the spine of the state of Oregon, running its length from north to south. Vast tracts of forest blanket the mountain slopes; snow-laden peaks poke above 10,000 feet. Storms rushing in from the Pacific Ocean are blocked by the mountains, stack up on them, and dump all their rain or snow on them. East of the mountains, lying in their rain-shadow, is a virtual desert.

The Deschutes, one of the world's few large north-flowing rivers, runs through this semi-arid land, parallel to the eastern flank of the Cascades. It gathers snow-melt streams and mountain run-off for almost the entire length of Oregon, and delivers the water into the Columbia River, which returns it to the Pacific—where the rain and snow originated.

A young river in geological terms, the Deschutes had an ancient predecessor that ran west, right into the ocean. But it was turned north and forced to cut a new course when the Cascades arose, only 3-4 million years ago. The river is still boisterous, full of bounce, and teeming with fish.

Shaped by nature and man

Two large irrigation impoundments, the Crane Prairie and Wickiup Reservoirs, now block the river in its forested headwater regions. These reservoirs offer excellent trophy trout fishing. Yet because of poorly regulated flows downstream, and creeping siltation, the dams have reduced fish populations in about 50 miles (80 kilometres) of the upper Deschutes River largely to hatchery trout. At the lower end of this stretch, in the middle region of the

river, it is blocked again by two hydroelectric power dams. However, the lower one, Pelton Dam, is re-regulating and serves to even out the discharge, stabilizing the lower river.

The lower Deschutes is the 100-mile (160-km) free-flowing river between Pelton Dam and the Columbia River. It is what we mean today by fishing the Deschutes. In a sense, the Deschutes is a "tailwater" river, with a dam providing its excellent fishing. But the river was always stabilized by a huge underground lava aquifer that captured run-off in spring, and released it through the summer more steadily than man has done. Before man rearranged it, the Deschutes was the most stable river of its size in the world, almost a giant—but not gentle—spring creek.

The lower river cuts through its young geography with a lot of energy. Its rapids are powerful, with high standing waves and frothed white water. The canyon walls are volcanic, layered and black, cliffed above the river or cascading down to it in tumbled rockslides. The sagebrush-lined banks of the river are steep, unstable and difficult to wade. Still, they are enormously productive of both insects and trout.

Varieties of fish

At one time, the lower Deschutes was stocked each year with hatchery trout. This stopped in the 1970s, and today the entire trout population of the rich lower river is a native strain of rainbow, called "redside" for the bold flash of red on its flanks and cheeks. These are wild fish, averaging 1-2 pounds (0.5-1.0 kg) and often larger. They are strong and

know how to use the powerful river to propel their fighting.

Deschutes redsides are now protected by a slot limit: anglers are allowed to keep only two fish between 10 and 13 inches long (25-33 cm). This intelligent regulation has led to a bold increase in the numbers of trout at least 18 inches (45 cm) long, which weigh 3 lbs (1.5 kg) or more.

But the Deschutes is not just a trout stream. Summer steelhead enter it in mid-July, after leaving the ocean and swimming 200 miles (320 km) up the Columbia. They move upriver slowly and, by late September, are spread throughout the lower Deschutes to Pelton Dam. Averaging 5-6 lbs (2.2-2.7 kg) and often reaching 10-12 lbs (4.5-5.5 kg), they are active, willing to lift up and chase after a fly on the swing. They take with brutal thuds under the surface, or with great detonations on top of it. And

like the river's trout, these steelhead know how to use the currents as fuel for their fights.

Fishing the trout

My favorite way to fish the Deschutes is to float along it in a rubber raft or drift boat, and camp alongside it. The reason is simple: you haven't experienced the river until you've felt it toss you around. But here is a warning: unless you are an expert at whitewater boating, hire a guide to handle the oars. The Deschutes is dangerous, and it drowns several of the careless every year.

The structure of the Deschutes is not the typical riffle-run-pool of a more mature river. Instead, it has long runs, far too deep and powerful to wade, interspersed with occasional rapid or vast expanses of vigorous and insect-rich riffle. The riffle corners—right where the fast water first breaks over into water where trout can hold, and an angler can wade—are the most productive places in the river.

They hold trout constantly. I like to fish them with small weighted nymphs and strike indicators in the morning and evening. At midday, when insects are active, trout can easily be coaxed up to strike a dry fly.

My favorite trout fishing, though, is along the bouldery banks of those long runs. Fishing from a boat is forbidden on the Deschutes: you have to tie up and fish on foot. If you are willing to work your way into difficult places, you find lots of trout, and some large ones. The banks are best fished by rock-hopping on the shore when possible, and wading carefully along the steep edges where necessary. Cast high-floating dry flies, like the Elk Hair Caddis, into indentations in the shoreline and up under sweeping alder trees. Trout will dash up, take with a splash, turn downstream and instantly pull you into your backing.

Some popular flies for Deschutes trout are the Box Canyon Stone Nymph and Improved Sofa Pillow dry (both of size 6-8, during the salmon fly hatch in late May and early June), the Stimulator dry (size 6-10, during the Golden Stone hatch in June), and the Elk or Deer Hair Caddis (size 12-16) for the summer months when caddis go crazy along the banks. For nymphing riffles through the season, Gold-Ribbed Hare's Ear, Pheasant Tail, Fox Squirrel, and Muskrat Nymphs of size 14-16 are recommended. Use split shot to get the fly down, and a strike indicator to tell when a fish takes.

The best season to fish the Deschutes for trout is in spring and early summer—April through early July. On the other hand, steelhead fishing is best in August and September. In October you can fish them both on a combination trip, but bad weather is a possibility then.

Surprising steelhead

Steelhead hold in the riffles and in long shallow flats. The ideal fly water is 2-6 feet (about 1-2 metres) deep, with a well-featured riverbed and a current that is pushy but not too strong to wade. You've got to be patient. Cast a No. 4-8 Green Butt Skunk, Fall Favorite or Silver Hilton, letting it swing down and across the current: step and cast, step and cast. Being light-shy, the steelhead are best fished at dawn and dusk. It can take hours to get that first strike—but when you do, the fight of the steelhead quickly makes it worth the wait.

The most exciting aspect of the Deschutes is its ability to surprise. The quick strike of a large trout to a dry fly is always astonishing, even when you can predict the moment it will happen. So is the sudden thud of a steelhead intercepting your fly, then shouldering away to leap high with it.

But the least expected of all is the instant when a steelhead detonates on your trout fly, tied to its fragile tippet. Then you have a problem on your hands. You won't often solve it, but you're sure to have plenty of excitement trying. ✿

The North Umpqua

Clayne F. Baker

This is one of America's greatest steelhead rivers, beloved for its beauty and picturesque setting. It lies northeast of Roseberg, Oregon, on Highway 138. There are steelhead and spring chinook salmon in the river from April through October, but the best steelhead fishing is from May through July.

Flyfishing paradise

If you have had the good fortune to visit Oregon, west of the Cascade Mountains, you probably know that the storms sweeping in from the Pacific Ocean in winter collide with the Cascade Mountain Range, painting the western slopes of Oregon a rich, rain-forest green. Stands of Douglas fir, dressed in their darkest olive, rise above a blanket of shrubs, plants and ferns. The tree trunks and branches hang heavy with moss, many being choked with mistletoe.

The coast of Oregon, from the California border north to that of Washington, has hundreds of clear-flowing rivers, big and small, winding their way through this jungle of greenery to spill their sweet water into the salty Pacific. Each stream has its own personality and beauty, and their steelhead strains differ genetically. Throughout the year, salmon and steelhead ascend these rivers, returning to where they were born.

Anglers who know the rivers of Oregon consider the North Umpqua to be the crown jewel of the state's steelhead rivers. It originates near Maidu Lake and Diamond Lake, high in the Cascades. For a hundred miles (160 kilometres) it races through a steep, forested canyon like a raging bull. From Rock

Creek—west of Steamboat Inn—to Mott's Bridge, the river is open to flyfishing only.

A 400-yard portion of the river near the confluence of Steamboat Creek, called "the Camp Water", is a series of 25 pools, resembling a necklace of emeralds when seen from the air. This water attracts flyfishermen from all over the world. In 1986 the North Umpqua was designated the best river on the Oregon coast for summer steelhead. Today's runs far surpass the numbers in the river's recorded history.

A favorite river

Stone Age people, and later the Umpqua Indian tribe, lived an idyllic primitive life in the river's valley. The Indian word "Umpqua" is interpreted as "high and low water", or as an Indian call meaning "Boat, bring over water!" The Umpqua folk, shy and reserved, avoided the white fur trappers who moved into their valley, refusing to trade goods. Each spring the Indians tracked salmon and steelhead up the river, where they had a fishing camp at Narrow Falls near Rock Creek. Here they speared fish from platforms over the narrow basalt channels. They also fished with seines and baskets, and trapped fish in the tributary creeks in weirs.

Fishing camps on the North Umpqua were first established in the 1920s. Major Jordon Lawrence Mott opened a fishing camp and guide service in 1929. During the early 1930s, the famous novelist Zane Grey was a regular visitor to the North Fork of the Umpqua. Grey's books about cowboys and the Wild West outsold every book except the Bible

and McGuffey's Readers. His vast wealth allowed him to fish or hunt anywhere in the world. In 1935, he wrote in a article about the North Umpqua in *Sports Afield:* "Its fishing is superior to any river in the United States, and comparable only to the great rivers of Newfoundland or the far-famed Tongariro of New Zealand." Many of the pools on the river near Steamboat Lodge were named by Grey and his family, including Ledges, Divide Pool, Split Rock Hole, and Takahashi Pool (named after Grey's cook).

Floating-line fishing

Today's North Umpqua is different than it was when Zane Grey fished there, or when Major Mott guided flyfishermen to the holes far from the nearest road. In the 1930s, much of the quality water was

accessible only by rough gravel roads. Now the river can be reached on Highway 138 from Roseberg, Oregon.

The historic Steamboat Inn is the shrine for flyfishing visitors. This lodge was built by Clarence Gordon in 1935 on a bluff overlooking perhaps the finest stretch on the river. Guests enjoy the tradition of excellence in an atmosphere of the past, and are surprised with a variety of gourmet meals that rival the West's finest restaurants.

The North Fork is a small river, and the water is so clear that you can often fish for an individual fish. The road follows the river for many miles and is elevated above it, so an angler using polaroid glasses or binoculars can spot the steelhead in the mint-green pools. This is also a very difficult river to wade, and the clear water can fool you: three feet of depth can prove to be six. Flat rocks on the bottom often feel

used—including the Umpqua and the Surveyor streamers, both featured in Ray Bergman's book *Trout* (1944). Zane Grey fished the Parmachene Bell and the Hair Coachman, among other flies, during his reign on the river. Today's visitors cast flies like the Montana Girdle Bug and rabbit-hair leeches, with bodies of black or purple Crystal Chenille. Dry flies can also be effective, such as the October Caddis, the Bomber, Muddler, and Wulff hairwing patterns.

Not only do I dream about the Umpqua: I am haunted by it. I know of no other stream that draws me more than this sweet water does. I look forward to dining at the Steamboat Inn, listening to stories of what the river was like in the old days. I can explore its pools and riffles with a streamer fly, perhaps watched by the ghosts of Major Mott, Zane Grey and Ray Bergman. And if I am lucky, I will witness the bright silver Umpqua steelhead, with a back of pure steel, as it throws its lithe gleaming body into the air. ✺

as if they were greased, and there are ledges that slip away into deep underwater caverns.

The fishing is done mostly with a floating line. Flyfishermen swim their flies through the slots in the tailouts of the pools before they crash over to become rapids. Historic streamer patterns are still

Camping grounds exist throughout the North Fork of the Umpqua area. Lodging and superb dining are offered by the Steamboat Inn, overlooking some of the river's finest water.

The Snake River

Erwin A. Bauer

This is one of the great trout rivers born in Yellowstone Park. But unlike the others, which flow north, the Snake first flows southward for about 100 miles (160 kilometres). Then it loses its identity in the Palisades Reservoir and eventually joins the Columbia River, which empties into the Pacific Ocean.

For much of that distance it flows within sight of, if not exactly in the shadow of, Wyoming's Teton Mountain range. The Grand, the tallest of the Teton peaks, rises abruptly 7,000 feet (2,100 metres) above mile-high Jackson Hole and the Snake.

Magnificent surroundings

Few if any other trout rivers in the world pass through such a wonderful scene for such a great distance. Whenever I am on this river, my mind wanders to the high mountain trails and to the lonely trout lakes in unseen glacial valleys far above me. The moose and elk, beavers, otters and bald eagles that one meets along the Snake in Grand Teton National Park can be a welcome distraction.

Generally speaking, the Snake River is much more productive and pleasant to fly-cast late in the summer than early. If winter snowfall is normal, waterflow the next spring will be high and turbid. The uppermost 20 miles (32 km) usually become clear and wadable by mid-July. Below that, where large stretches of water are reachable only by foot-trail, the prime fishing does not begin until late July, but it lasts into October when the cottonwoods and quaking aspens along the bank have turned a luminous

yellow. Then it is excellent dry-fly water, and the favourite fly patterns are Humpies, Royal Wulffs and Royal Trudes in sizes 10-14.

Midway on its course into Grand Teton Park, the Snake passes through Jackson Lake, an artificial impoundment for distant irrigation—which never should have been built. Periodically some heavy trout are caught in the tailwaters of Jackson Dam. Downstream from there, the rest of the river is best fished from a float-boat. Wading is not impossible, but the current is deceptively swift and the bottom is slick enough to be dangerous. In addition, drifting downstream with a guide who is also a skillful boat handler allows the angler to cover more water easily. Launch and access sites exist at one-day float-trip intervals all along the way, from Dead Man's Bar to Moose and the Snake River Bridge.

Barbless hooks

Fall fishing can be the liveliest of all. That is when a large weighted nymph is very effective. Muddlers and other streamer flies produce very well in the long, smooth runs and deep pools. I favor a Geriatric Muddler, my own creation—a regular muddler fly, but with white wings that make it easier for older fishermen to fix on a fine leader.

Actually the river described above should be called the South Fork of the Snake. After disappearing in the Palisades Reservoir southwest of Jackson, it re-emerges in southeastern Idaho and flows for another 40-50 miles (65-80 km) before becoming a warm-water stream. The parts I like best are from

Renowned stretches

Mike Dawson—a premier fishing guide of Island Park, Idaho—is among the many who regard the Henry's (or North) Fork of the Snake River as the "promised land" for serious trout anglers. He points to its exquisite mountain setting, to the amazing number and diversity of its insect hatches, and to its large but very selective trout. In addition, the Henry's Fork flow is cold and constant, its bed is easy to wade, and strict regulations exist to ensure quality fishing far into the future.

Henry's Fork begins high up at Henry's Lake—itself a trophy trout fishery—and in Big Spring, a trout sanctuary where you can watch rainbow up to 10 lbs (4.5 kg) swimming and feeding in the transparent water that issues from underground. Downstream, the Henry's Fork offers a variety of fishing waters that can make an addict of an otherwise normal sportsman.

Consider first a 3-mile (5-km) section called Box Canyon, from Island Park Reservoir to Last Chance. Its cobblestone bottom and nearly vertical, brushy banks make it an ordeal to reach. But the salmon fly hatches are so large in midsummer and the fish so heavy, that many fishermen tackle it anyway.

The best method is to travel downstream by boat, anchoring in order to wade at a few safe places along the way. The water below Mesa Falls is similar to Box Canyon and also holds many trout.

By far the most celebrated water of Henry's Fork is the 6-mile (10-km) stretch within Harriman State

Palisades dam for about 12 miles (20 km) to Swan Valley, and the longer stretch from Swan Valley to near Heise Hot Springs.

On all of this territory, barbless hooks are required, to maintain the high quality of the fishing. The upper half can be waded easily; farther down, a boat is best. The most successful local anglers use dry flies (Sofa Pillows, Humpies), weighted nymphs (Box Canyon or Montana Stones) or streamers (muddlers, spuddlers or zonkers) as the season progresses.

Park, better known locally as Railroad Ranch. In total contrast to Box Canyon, this is a smooth stream averaging 300 feet (90 metres) wide, easily waded. Vegetation grows lush and waves in the sinuous current. Rainbow trout are almost always rising actively, and at times there seem to be whole schools of them feeding on the myriad insects.

Huge hatches

Name a native Western aquatic insect—it probably lives here. Among the common hatches (and flies to match them) on Railroad Ranch are Pale Morning Duns, Green Drakes, Trico and Blue-Wing Olives. The hungry trout also feed on terrestrials: grasshoppers, beetles, and ants fallen or blown in from the grassy banks. The most successful fisherman is the one who consistently best matches any given hatch. But refined tackle, a cautious approach by stalking, and a soft presentation of the fly downstream, are just as important.

To be honest, the Henry's Fork can be as maddening as it is classic flyfishing water. Like so many kindred spirits, I have waded for hours with splendid trout rising all around, but without a rise to my own fly. However, I am more inclined to remember the cool, dewy morning when I hooked three heavy rainbows in just that many casts, netting only the third one.

All flies used on Henry's Fork must be barbless, and at present only one trout over 20 inches (50 cm) can be retained. But there is an unwritten rule here, generally observed, that every trout caught must be promptly and gently released.

The U.S. Forest Service maintains public camping grounds along Henry's Fork throughout the fishing season. There are also motels nearby at Island Park, Last Chance and Mack's Inn.

The Madison River

Erwin A. Bauer

Late on a cool, golden evening in 1870, a band of weary explorers huddled around a campfire at the end of a difficult but extraordinary journey. For more than a month, General Henry Washburn—surveyor general of Montana Territory—had led them on foot and horseback across a trackless wilderness, where none of the men could truly comprehend what he saw.

Hot spring boiled violently and geysers exploded from underground. Grizzly bears and wolves stalked high mountain meadows where great rivers were born. Everywhere the scenery was magnificent. From their campfire, the travellers could see where two of these rivers (today called the Gibbon and Firehole) joined to form a large waterway, later to be named the Madison.

To a man, the explorers were so awed by their experience that they agreed that this remarkable wilderness should be saved—set aside and never settled—for all the American people forever. It was a radical thought for the times. Soon afterward, in 1872, President Ulysses S. Grant designated Yellowstone as the country's (and the world's) first national park. Thus, too, a couple of major "dream waters", the Madison and Yellowstone Rivers, were preserved unspoilt and pure for future generations.

Three Madisons

The Madison is by no means classic trout water, but it is usually very productive before the peak high water (from snow run-off) until midsummer. In statistical terms, this is probably Montana's most reliable trout river. Year in and year out, it is also the most popular, being fishable along its entire 120 miles (192 kilometres). But serious anglers regard the Madison as three separate rivers. The first Madison includes the 15 miles (25 km) from its origin in Yellowstone Park to the western park boundary. Rainbow trout dominate the 50-mile (75-km) middle section—the second Madison—from Yellowstone to Ennis Lake and Beartrap Canyon. Downstream to Three Rivers, where the Madison joins the Gallatin and Jefferson Rivers (both excellent trout waters) to form the mighty Missouri, is mostly brown trout water. This third Madison is favored by many trophy hunters.

For me, the first Madison has a mystique that is difficult to match, especially in September and October. Whereas fishing by boat (float tripping) is the best way to fish the rest of the river, only wading is permitted here. The main Yellowstone Park road closely parallels the Madison, and I can pause wherever I like, then walk to a promising bend or riffle. Perhaps nowhere else on earth is so much blue-ribbon trout-fishing water so easily accessible, and free to the public.

However, there are distractions such as the trumpeter swans, Canada geese, and curious otters that share the river. It is often hard to concentrate on rising trout, when bull elk are bugling and gathering harems of cows in the meadows all round. Both the sights and sounds are spectacular. An angler might also meet a bison grazing at the water's edge.

Challenges

Some of the first Madison's best places are the Seven and Nine Mile holes, the National Park Meadows, Barnes Hole, Big Bend, Grasshopper Bank, and Beaver Meadow—all restricted to flyfishing only. But the heaviest trout are wary, and the footing in some of these places is extremely slippery. So I always wade cautiously, wear waders with felt soles and carry a wading staff.

Whereas the opposite ends of the Madison offer the greatest challenge to a fisherman, as well as the biggest trout, the middle section—the long riffle—is an ideal spot for beginners, or anyone simply seeking action instead of heavy trout. Here the river is more forgiving to inexpert casting than the "flat", placid sections may be. The trout tend to be smaller and less shy than elsewhere. The average current

speed, 5 mph (8 km/h), means that a fish must take or leave a fly before it is swept out of range.

Fishing is also very consistent in the 30 miles (50 km) between Quake Lake and McAtee Bridge, where all trout must be released alive. The famous salmon fly hatch begins about July 1 on the Madison's lower reaches, and gradually moves upstream for 3-4 weeks. There are days during this period when salmon fly imitations, such as Sofa Pillows and Fluttering Stones, produce almost non-stop action.

Troubles

Many hard-core anglers in Montana prefer to fish the lower—or third—Madison below Ennis and Beartrap Canyon, where the best seasons are April-June and in autumn until it becomes too cold for

comfort. And no wonder, because brown trout up to 12 lbs (5.5 kg) have been taken here, and specimens of 4-5 lbs (2 kg) are not rare. There are also good rainbow trout deep in the 7-mile (11-km) Beartrap Canyon, but this requires a guided whitewater float trip by inflatable rubber raft. Just running the wild water safely here does not allow much chance to concentrate on fishing. But the Beartrap voyage itself is exciting, and an excellent way to cool off on a hot August afternoon.

Besides the abundant trout, another factor makes exploring the Madison River (as well as the Snake and Yellowstone, described elsewhere in this book) an unadulterated pleasure. In all of this high country, the weather is generally cool, sunny, dry and exhilarating throughout the fishing season. Occasionally in summer a hot wind does blow, but rain and overcast days are rare. It is truly dream-water country.

A visitor to the Madison River region today finds plenty of public camping grounds, motels, and dude or guest-ranch accommodations available. Commercial air service flies into West Yellowstone and Bozeman, Montana. There are tackle shops in West Yellowstone and Ennis, where the information is up-to-date, professional guides can be found, and the international language of trout fishing is fluently spoken! ✻

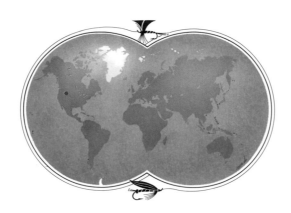

The Yellowstone River

Erwin A. Bauer

The longest undammed trout stream on Earth is probably still the Yellowstone of Wyoming and Montana. A serious flyfisherman might devote his entire life to this river alone, without really covering every pool and pocket in its trout-bearing length of at least 300 miles (500 kilometres).

Virgin waters

Not until the early nineteenth century did the first non-Indian lay eyes on the Yellowstone. In 1807, restless John Colter took leave of the Lewis & Clark Expedition (the first one that crossed the United States to the Pacific Ocean) and did some wandering on his own. Colter may also have been the first fisherman on the Yellowstone. But it was Jim Bridger, the beaver trapper and legendary mountainman, who first described the river to a large audience. His extravagant tales, some true and others exaggerated, of this magnificent country and region are retold even today.

Nobody believed Bridger's account of catching a trout in the cold river and simply turning around to cook it in a boiling hot spring. Yet that tale was probably true, and the same feat could be performed today.

The Yellowstone originates just beneath the continental divide, a mile and a half above sea level in the Teton Wilderness, about 20 miles (30 kilometres) southeast of Yellowstone National Park. From its birthplace, it hurries generally north toward Yellowstone Lake. Far from any roads, this stretch is fished by only a few anglers every season, because it must

be reached by arduous hiking or by several days on horseback. But I can testify that the almost virgin fishing is well worth the time, expense and sore muscles. Here in early summer may be the best fishing in the world for one species: Yellowstone blackspotted cutthroat trout.

Continuing downstream, the river enters Yellowstone Lake and meets its first auto road. Suddenly the fishing pressure is heavy. But although fly anglers must compete here with trollers in boats and spincasters on shore, fishing with a light rod can still be worthwhile near daybreak and dusk.

The cutthroat

From Yellowstone Lake northward, the river again belongs to flyfishermen only. Through Hayden Valley it is a classic meadow stream, where the cutthroats rise willingly on summer evenings, and wildlife watching is part of the game. Occasionally, as when a herd of a hundred bison fords the river too nearby, it is hard to concentrate on the trout. The park's main loop road closely parallels the river through this valley.

North of Hayden Valley, the river plunges suddenly—with two spectacular, thundering falls—into the Grand Canyon of the Yellowstone. Steep trails make it possible to fish on the floor of the canyon, but it is advisable to pass up this turbulent 24-mile (38-km) stretch. However, be sure to enjoy the awesome view of the incredibly coloured canyon

walls before you proceed. Artist's Point is one of several convenient vantage points.

For many dedicated flyfishermen, the Yellowstone river does not really begin until it leaves Wyoming near the town of Gardiner, Montana (where inflow from the Gardiner and Lamar rivers almost doubles its size), or from just below Yankee Jim Canyon. Until this point, the trout are native cutthroats; but from here northward, introduced rainbows and browns predominate.

Boat fishing

Usually the middle Yellowstone has the best fishing. It is no wonder that this part of the state is known as Paradise Valley.

The upstream 42 miles (67 km) of Paradise Valley, from Gardiner down to an access point known as Mallard's Rest, is a splendid blend of slow and fast water—as challenging to "read" as to cast on. Further downstream, for another 30 miles (50 km) from Mallard's Rest to below Livingston, the river picks up speed and the trout are larger on average, if not quite as abundant.

Throughout Paradise Valley, fishing by boat is best, and public boat-launching sites are located at regular intervals all along the way. However, some worthwhile wading is also possible around the access sites. Trout can be caught downstream from Livingston for another 60 miles (100 km) or so, to about Columbus, Montana. But at that point the Yellowstone subtly changes from a cold-water (trout) fishery to a warm-water fishery.

In Paradise Valley the river is open to fishing year round. Even in midwinter, when temperatures fall below 0°F and the waterway is partly encrusted in ice, a few hardy anglers are busy casting tiny midge (locally called snow fly) imitations. Mostly they catch whitefish, which are delicious when smoked, but some large trout are also netted.

The caddis and mayfly hatches are uncountable during a typical spring-through-fall season. The largest hatch on the river is the giant salmon fly in July. Unlike the strategy on other waters, most fishermen do not always try to match these hatches; instead they rely on such attractive patterns as the Humpy, Royal Wulff, Goofus Bug or Trude. For fishing deep water along the bottom, I keep a supply of Spruce flies, muddlers or other sculpin-like streamers in my fishing vest. Experts often depend on Elk Hair Caddis flies, Woolly Worms, and a Bitch Creek or similar weighted nymph.

The higher the water level, the better it is to boat-fish than to wade, because the best fish hold close to the banks. Preferred tackle is slightly on the heavy side, with nine-foot rods in AFTM class 7-8 for dry flies, or in class 9-10 for streamers and larger nymphs.

Big trout

No essay on the Yellowstone is complete without mentioning the two beautiful spring creeks, Armstrong and Nelson, which bubble clear as crystal from beneath Paradise Valley about 10 miles (16 km) south of Livingston. Both are private streams containing lush vegetation, a bewildering population of insects and plenty of well-fed, heavy trout.

It is hard to stay "cool" with such fish rising all about. Of course, very delicate tackle and presentation are needed to tempt them. Only a limited number of fishermen are allowed each day on these streams, to maintain quality and "elbow room".

Except possibly during the peak of the tourist season in Yellowstone Park (mid-July until the end of August) when reservations may be advisable, accommodations are readily available in Livingston, Gardiner and the Park (Mammoth, Canyon and Lake areas). Bailey's Tackle Shop can normally arrange for a guide and boat on a day's notice. The nearest commercial air service is at Billings or Bozeman, Montana. ⚶

The Bighorn River

Dave Hughes

*I*n north-central Wyoming, the Wind River—having gathered all of its tributaries—enters a canyon and emerges a few miles later. Just after that, it passes into south-central Montana, with a new name: the Bighorn. This is one of the few rivers in the world which changes its name in mid-course, for no apparent reason.

Until 1968, the Bighorn was silted and warm, offering little trout fishing. Then the Yellowtail Dam was built, and the reservoir behind it serves as a settling basin for silt. Its depth cools the water to trout-stream temperatures all year round. The river below the dam is clean and rich in suspended nutrients, promoting rooted plants. These shelter and feed a myriad of insects and crustaceans, which in turn feed a heavy population of brown and rainbow trout.

Fishing below the dam

The Bighorn tailwater meanders peacefully for 70 miles (110 kilometres) across Montana's south-central plain, eventually flowing into the Yellowstone River. Only the first 30 miles (50 km) downstream from the dam allow trout fishing. Below that, it reverts to a warm-water fishery.

In fact, the fishable stretch extends only to 13 miles (20 km) below the dam, where a tributary adds muddy irrigation water to the river during part of the year. This inflow—when at its worst, for most of the summer—clouds the rest of the good trout water downstream. Trout still hold in those lower reaches, but they do not respond well to hatches of insects, and are most likely to be taken with streamers.

The good stretch may not sound very long, but the river is so broad and rich that it provides a lot of superb trout fishing—even when it gets crowded, as it does at times. In this fishable area, the water is flat and flows through beautiful cottonwood bottoms, in a valley that is even wider and flatter.

There are no significant rapids, but many long and productive riffles and flats where the trout seem to feed constantly in pods. They bounce up little columns of spray when feeding in the riffles, and on the flats they feed daintily with sipping rise-forms. It is not uncommon to cast over rising trout all day on the Bighorn. Few of its fish are smaller than 14 inches (35 cm). Some trout in the pods weigh 3-4 pounds (around 1.5 kg), causing problems when your leader is tapered fine enough to fool them.

The best time to be on the Bighorn is May or June, before the weather heats up—or September and October, after it cools off. In midsummer the fishing can be excellent, especially on nymphs, but hot weather may hold back the hatches.

Preferable nymph patterns are No. 14-18 Pheasant Tails, Fox Squirrel Nymphs, and Olive Scuds. San Juan Worms, in size 8-12, also work well. For dries, try No. 16-20 Blue-Wing Olives in either Compara-Dun or Hair-Wing Dun styles. When trout are on Pale Morning Duns, try a size 16-18 yellowish-olive Compara-Dun or Hair-Wing Dun. If the trout sip midges in eddies and backwaters, a size 16-22 Griffith's Gnat might take them. Hatches of spotted sedges can be matched with a No. 14-16 Deer Hair Caddis. Dark American grannons are matched with a No. 16-20 Dark Elk Hair Caddis.

Different ways of fishing

The river flows through a combination of private property and the Crow Indian Reservation, where trespassing is forbidden. There are three points of access to the river on its fishable stretch; you can easily walk and fish a mile or two upstream or down from each of them. Hiking is a fine way to fish this part of the river, but the most pleasant way is by boat. Floating opens up many miles of water that you would not otherwise be able to reach. It separates you from the occasional crowd. And it's the only way to fish downstream from the last of the three access points. There are no others for almost 20 miles (32 km).

The Bighorn is fished by two methods that both work well, but offer different kinds of satisfaction. The first is with nymphs, using split shot to get them down and a strike indicator to help detect takes. Because the river is so rich with insects and scuds, trout feed along the bottom almost constantly in the long riffles and runs. Most people wade when fishing nymphs. But many guides get clients to fish by simply directing them to cast nymphs off the bow and stern, then watch their strike indicators drift downstream, apace with the boat. This doesn't take much skill, and never takes long to yield the joy of seeing an indicator dip under water.

The second method—and there is no better place in the world for it than the Bighorn—is to look for rising trout and match the insects they are taking. It is not always easy; the hatches are sometimes an intricate puzzle, and the fish are always fussy. But there is no greater reward than solving a hatch over selective brown trout that average 15 inches (38 cm) and are often a lot bigger.

A typical experience of my own was the first day I floated the Bighorn, and in the end it made me wish I had walked. With a friend, I launched a drift boat just below the dam at mid-morning. We drifted from pod to pod of rising trout until late afternoon. Suddenly my companion pointed out that darkness was only two hours away, with ten miles to go! We had been fishing the first three miles of water all day, happily casting and always taking just enough trout to keep us interested.

We then took turns at the oars and tried to dash down to the takeout. But we arrived exhausted long after dark. The lesson was that one should move faster from pod to pod, and get some early miles under the keel, so that one is closer to the takeout when light begins to fade. But it's hard to stop fishing when the trout are still rising, and we continue to

feel our way tentatively down the final stretch in the dark whenever we visit the Bighorn.

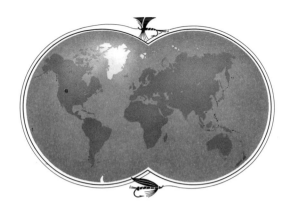

The Firehole River

Dave Hughes

The Firehole flows through Yellowstone Park, in the state of Wyoming. It is a land of geothermal anxieties, with mudpots bubbling and seething near the river. Fumaroles toss up steam and sulfur. Old Faithful Geyser, at the river's head, arises majestically every hour, a tall column of hot water escaping from underground pressures, trying to turn itself into a cloud. Some hot springs emerge in the riverbed itself, and there are said to be places where you can cook trout only a few feet from where you hook them. I haven't tried it, but I believe it.

Food aplenty

The river itself is a spring creek, emerging from the ground as clear as air. It meanders for about 15 miles (25 kilometres) through geyser basins and jackpine forests to its junction with the upper Madison River. At first narrow, little more than a cast across, it grows as it gathers springs, and is broad though still shallow in the last few miles. Its bottom is stable lava rock, and you can wade it in most areas without danger.

Because its flows are stable, the Firehole River has lots of rooted vegetation, with congregations of small mayfly nymphs, caddis-fly larvae, and scuds. Trout in the Firehole, both browns and rainbows, average 10-15 inches (25-38 cm) long. They feed on abundant insect hatches, and are fished intensely in the areas closest to roads.

These trout can be so selective that you might think they had college degrees in entomology. The fishing is challenging, but also rewarding: when you fool a Firehole fish, you know you've accomplished an excellent deception. The fish you fool won't always be small, either. In autumn, when brown trout make a spawning run out of Hebgen Lake and up through the Madison River into the Firehole, you may be surprised by a fish in the 3-lb (1.4-kg) class or even bigger.

I prefer to fish the sections that meander away from roads, although one can often drive on the roads parallel to the river and spot rising trout from the car. It surprises me that most people fish within sight of their cars, neglecting water that takes a walk of only a quarter or half mile. So I wear lightweight waders, tuck a lunch in my cargo pocket and a bamboo rod under my arm, then meander through the meadows and the pines along the river.

Imitations

Much of the Firehole is apparently too shallow to hold fish. But the lava flats and weedbeds actually have hidden trenches and shelves, where trout can hide and slip out to feed when hatches occur. All of the river's bends have undercut banks, and wherever a tree has fallen across the current, trout find sheltered lies among the limbs. It's best to slip along the river quietly and slowly, watching the water constantly for signs of feeding fish.

A third of the battle is stalking into a good position for casting without scaring the trout. Another third is figuring out what insect the trout are taking, and what kind of fly might match it. And the last third is making a presentation that tricks the trout.

Hatches are almost always tiny on the Firehole, and your fly box should offer a wide selection of dressings in sizes 16-22.

Hatches

There are, however, times when the hatch is not small. For example, during the grasshopper season in July, August and early September, you will do well with size 10-14 flies, and often best when you drop them onto the water with a smack. But again, many terrestrials are tiny. I have seen fish feeding with delicate rises under grasses overhanging the water, and spent hours before realizing that they were rising to minute beetles which fell on the water. Once this was clear, catching the trout became easy.

Perhaps the most difficult Firehole hatches to comprehend are caddis. You see adults dancing in the air and dapping to the water, especially near eve-

ning. Trout rise, seemingly taking them from the surface. Yet your dry flies go unharmed. Try fishing very small, soft-hackled wet flies of size 16-20, when you see caddis hatching on the Firehole, and your luck might change surprisingly.

Techniques

Standard nymphing tactics, with split shot and a bright strike indicator, will work on the Firehole, but only in water that is deep and vigorous enough to keep the indicator from spooking trout. Normally it is best to use a nymph that is slightly weighted, leaving off the shot or adding just a micro-shot, and to use a small segment of yarn on the leader as an unobtrusive indicator, rather than one which floats like a bobber and astonishes the fish.

The best season on the Firehole is from early June through October. The fishing slows somewhat, and

moves to morning and evening, in the hot days of late July and August. Small flies are best; for nymphs, try standards such as the Gold-Ribbed Hare's Ear, Zug Bug, Olive Scud, and Squirrel Nymph, tied on No. 14-20 hooks. Weight them slightly so that you can fish them without split shot in shallow, clear water.

Soft-hackled wet flies solve caddis problems on the Firehole from time to time. Try such standards as the No. 16-20 Partridge and Yellow, Partridge and Green, or Grouse and Orange.

For dry flies, try the Adams and Blue-Wing Olive in No. 16-20, but also arm yourself with a selection of small flies that match hatches: the Little Olive Compara-Dun and Blue-Wing Olive Hairwing Dun in No. 16-20, and the Griffith's Gnat in No. 18-22. A Letort Hopper in No. 10-14 will take trout during the hot grasshopper season. ❧

Henry's Lake

Clayne F. Baker

This large, shallow lake lies in the southeast corner of Idaho, 18 miles (30 km) southwest of West Yellowstone, Montana. It is famous for big hybrid rainbow/cutthroat trout, as well as for cutthroat and trophy-sized brook trout. Nestled at the foot of the Centennial Mountains, surrounded by mountain meadows and bordered by a forest of lodge pole pine and Douglas fir, it can well be called a dream lake.

By late spring its bottom is a jungle of aquatic plants. These and the superb quality of fresh water—populated by shrimp, lake caddis, dragonfly and damselfly nymphs, chironomids and leeches—makes Henry's Lake a trout factory with few equals. It has been a popular fishing place for over a century, and offers perhaps the best opportunity in the western United States to catch a trophy brook trout or a rainbow/cutthroat hybrid.

Major Henry

In July 1810, Major Andrew Henry and his party of 50-80 trappers were harassed by Blackfoot warriors near Three Forks on the Missouri River in Montana. Choosing a southern route to avoid further contact with the Indians, they crossed the continental divide near the Targee Pass and arrived at this lake. Major Henry gave his name to it, and to the river he followed for days—"Henry's Fork of the Snake".

Major Henry also established Fort Henry near the present town of Ashton, Idaho. The trappers occupied the lonely fort for two years. Many suffered from snow blindness and, at one time, some even "begged to be shot". They survived the second winter only by eating their horses, and 27 died or were killed during the expedition.

Managing the lake

The lake's native fish is the Henry's Lake cutthroat trout. Eastern brook trout were introduced in 1922, and the state record "brookie" of 7 lbs 2 oz (3.2 kg) was caught here in 1978. In 1950 the Idaho Fish and Game Department implanted cutthroat/rainbow hybrids, which grew to trophy size. Strong and acrobatic, these hybrids have reached weights of 18 lbs (8 kg).

This Department—along with the Henry's Lake Foundation, an association of sportsmen—has also worked on stream rehabilitation projects, to repair fish habitats by fencing and by planting trees along the spawning tributaries. In 1987, Temiscamie brook trout, a Canadian strain, was introduced. Indications are that these new brookies are growing in weight and wisdom, and could reach trophy size in the next few years.

Float-tube fishing

The trout fishing begins on May 26 and ends on November 30. It is best to fish in October and November, although snow can come early at Henry's Lake. Hundreds of fishing boats cover the lake throughout the season. By about the third week in June, the trolling lanes are closed off by weed growth, and the boat fishermen have to move to the open areas around the underwater springs.

Henry's Lake is home water to the famous "Idaho Float Tube Navy" (a nickname for Idaho anglers who have popularized flyfishing from a float tube). On summer days, the lake is spangled with hundreds of multicolored float tubes. Angling writer Pete Hidy called this scene "party fishing", since it is not unusual to see a dozen float-tubers side by side, close enough to carry on conversation.

Fly anglers cast a variety of lines to swim their nymphs over the weed beds. Slow to medium-sinking, and sink-tip, lines are popular, while deeper water requires fast-sinking lines. Popular fly patterns include shrimp imitations, leeches tied of marabou and mohair in brown, olive, gray, tan and black.

The damselfly hatch begins in early July. Hundreds of acrobatic nymphs migrate to the shallow water, where they climb the reeds, shedding their skin, and are reborn as adult damselflies. You will need damsel imitations with swimming fibres of marabou or ostrich tail to match this nymph.

In autumn, when the brook trout change to their rich spawning colours, streamer flies such as Mickey Finn or the Stayner Duck Tail will catch trout. An orange and black woolly bugger called the Halloween Leech, and the red mohair leech, are also effective at this time of year.

Morning fishing

My personal memories of Henry's Lake fishing trips go back twenty years. Trout that I have caught, and those that got away, swim in my thoughts. More than the fish, I remember the beauty of early mornings when the mist is still on the lake, with ghostly silhouettes of early-bird fishermen in boats and float tubes. I recall summer storms that sneak over the mountaintops without a whisper, then chase you off the lake with neon lances of lightning and explosions of thunder.

When October arrives, the aspen leaves are as yellow as daffodils and the breeze sweeping Henry's Lake has the taste of winter. I will be there just as last year, with my crazy float-tubing friends, all dressed like Eskimos to celebrate—in the best way we know—the end of this year's Idaho trout season. But I have made a resolution to come before the first ray of sunlight touches the mountains near the Targee Pass, where Major Henry first looked upon "his lake" so many years ago. After all, Bill Schiess wrote in his book, *Fishing Henry's Lake*, that the trophy brook trout quit biting before most fishermen get out of bed. ≿

Silver Creek

Clayne F. Baker

One of nature's most perfect trout streams, this giant spring creek lies about 30 miles (50 kilometres) south of Sun Valley, Idaho, the oldest ski resort in the United States. Its magic water, considered to be among the best in the country for dry-fly fishing, is born in a small valley between rolling hills, near the little towns of Gannett and Picabo. Hundreds of clear springs well up from the ground, forming streams that quickly unite to form a broad stream that meanders through the valley.

The bottom of Silver Creek is a jungle of waving aquatic plants that provide a home for vast numbers of freshwater shrimp, mayfly, caddis, leeches and so on. This rich food makes the fish grow large. Rainbows up to 28 inches (70 cm) are common, and there are some big brown trout and brookies in the cold feeder streams.

Beautiful rainbows

Before white men arrived, the Silver Creek valley was a popular hunting ground for the Indians. Marshy areas around the creek were alive with waterfowl and wading birds. At sunrise huge flocks of lumbering sagehen (some as large as turkeys) soared down from the surrounding hills for their morning drink of spring water. Buffalo herds visited the valley, and in the wooded draws were deer and elk. Cutthroat trout and Rocky Mountain whitefish, native to the stream, were probably speared and trapped by the Indians.

The first plantings of trout in Silver Creek came late in the nineteenth century. Several varieties of

rainbows, including a steelhead strain, were introduced. The McCloud strain of rainbows from northern California was planted in 1915. This trout prospered and, crossbreeding with existing strains, produced a lovely trout with distinctive spotting and colors. Silver Creek sportsmen found the rainbows superior to those in nearby waters.

In the 1930s, the stream was in prime condition; its water ran clear and cold. During the summer, watercress grew out into the stream, in some places covering it from bank to bank. Hidden under this umbrella, trout could feed without threat from their natural predators. Skilled flyfishermen were hard put

to make a dry-fly float, drag-free, for even a short distance in the narrow avenues between the watercress.

From 1930 to 1960, many of the marshes near the creek were drained and the soil cultivated. Barley, used to make beer, became the big money-crop; the farmers planted down to the banks of the stream. Suddenly the watercress disappeared and farm herbicides were blamed. Overgrazing by cattle in the upper reaches caused erosion and siltation.

The Sun Valley-Hollywood promotion and overuse of the creek between 1940 and 1950 added to the problems. Affluent flyfishermen flocked to the stream to fish for big rainbows. Fishing at Silver Creek declined. But in 1975 the finest portion, between Sullivan's Pond and Killpatrick Bridge, was bought by the Nature Conservancy, whose care has restored some of the stream's early splendor.

Extensive hatches

My first morning at Silver Creek was in June 1947. I waded into the creek apprehensively; it was still dark, and a cold breath of air swept along with the current. In my hand I held a Renegade dry fly, as I waited for the first light to dust the mountain peaks in the east. I could hear the sweet sounds of day-break: a quartet of frogs were performing at a sandbar downstream, ducks talked up and down the creek, and mudhens quarreled in the reeds.

I also heard fish rising nearby, as the sky brightened. Diamonds of light began to dance on the dark riffles. A cloud of insects surrounded me, and one ran across my face: it was a Silver Creek caddis hatch. Now I could see dozens of black noses sticking out of the water, and realized that I was standing smack in the middle of a trout-feeding frenzy! I offered my first cast, but after half an hour not a single trout had honored my fly.

Later that morning a tall young man dressed in jeans (no waders), a Western shirt and a cowboy hat, waded out to a small island above where I was casting. He had to pass through cold, shoulder-deep water, and I shuddered at his foolhardiness. He reached the island and disappeared, dripping, into the willows. That afternoon as I prepared to leave the stream, I heard a sound from the direction of the island. The smiling cowboy appeared and waded once again up to his shoulders in the water. At arm's length above his head he held the most handsome, red-sided rainbow trout that I had ever seen. It weighed over nine pounds (4 kg).

Today the creek is still cold and clear. The trout are strong, bright rainbows 10-28 inches (25-70 cm) long. In the lower reaches, a few big brown trout have found shelter in the deep holes and undercut banks.

The fishing season is from May 26 through November 31. Flyfishing is excellent all summer but, as on many Idaho streams, September and October are the choice months. There is a pale evening dun hatch at sunset from June to August, and brown drakes hatch in the evenings throughout June. Morning hatches of tiny tricorythodes sail downstream in late July through October. *Baetis* mayflies emerge in September and October.

Some winter evening when you settle into your bed to dream, shut your eyes and imagine rolling lavender hills surrounding a green valley with a wide stream of clear, cold currents dancing over emerald weedbeds. If you look closely, you may see a long olive shadow appear under your floating fly; the current is disturbed and your fly vanishes. Hang on, my friend!—you have hooked your first Silver Creek dream trout.

Camping grounds can be found in the nearby towns of Bellevue and Ketchum. Lodges, motels, condominiums, restaurants, fly shops and guide services are in Ketchum and Sun Valley.

Pyramid Lake

Clayne F. Baker

When the year moves toward winter, flyfishermen throughout the western United States dream of Pyramid Lake, 28 miles (45 kilometres) northeast of Reno, Nevada. From November to March, giant Lahontan cutthroat trout move out of the deep into shallow waters, preparing to spawn. They are a hardy strain, strong as a bulldog and tolerant to waters with high alkalinity. The Lahontan, a fierce predator, owes its amazing growth to millions of prolific tui-chubs that inhabit the lake.

Terrific trout

This special trout has ruled the lake since before the first Stone Age people found shelter in the caves along the shore. A National Park Service official wrote in 1947, "It is no exaggeration to say that Pyramid Lake is the most beautiful desert lake any member of the committee has yet seen—perhaps the most beautiful of its kind in North America."

On November 25, 1843, some 38 years after the Lewis & Clark Expedition to the Oregon Territory, explorer John Frémont and a party of 24 men left the Columbia River to explore the land to the southwest. They crossed a mountain pass and reached the northern end of a wonderful desert lake. Frémont wrote in his journal: "It was a sheet of green water, some 20 miles broad. It broke upon our eyes like the ocean. For a long time we sat enjoying the view, for we had become fatigued with the mountains." Three days later he wrote: "We camped on the shore opposite a very remarkable rock in the lake, which had attracted our attention for many miles. It rose, according to our estimate, 600 feet above the water and, from the point we viewed it, presented a pretty exact outline of the great pyramid of Cheops. This striking feature suggested a name for the lake, and I called it Pyramid Lake."

The following day, Frémont's party was met by a group of Indians who welcomed the explorers by catching giant trout for the travelers. Now he wrote: "The Indians were amused with our delight and immediately brought in numbers of trout. Their flavor was excellent—superior, in fact, to that of any fish I have ever known. They were of extraordinary size—about as large as the Columbia River salmon—generally fro two to four feet in length."

During the early 1900s, Pyramid Lake was a mecca for sportfishermen. On a windy December day in 1925, a Paiute Indian named John Skimmerhorn caught a 41-lb (19-kg) Lahontan cutthroat that is listed as the world record to this day. Pyramid Lake's popularity became paramount in the 1920s. President Herbert Hoover, actor Clark Gable, and sportsmen throughout the world came to fish for the big cutthroat.

Float-ring fishing

The trout fishing is open all year round, but the best time for big cutthroat is between January and April, when they move into shallow water. Today the lake offers perhaps the best opportunity in the world to catch a cutthroat trout of 5-20 lbs (2.3-9 kg) on an artificial fly.

The "line-up" at Pyramid Lake is one of the great

sights of American flyfishing. As many as thirty often stand in a row, hip deep in the lake, about 20 feet apart. They use long graphite rods and cast fast-sinking, shooting heads for maximum distance, with long bottom-hugging retrieves. Many of the regulars, mostly flyfishermen from nearby Reno, are at the lake several days of the week throughout winter. They frequently stand on metal milk-cases or aluminum ladders to allow longer casts.

Idaho flyfishermen, called the "Idaho Float Tube Navy", introduced float tubes to the big lake in the early 1970s and found them effective. Fishing with full-sinking, high-density lines, the float-tubers work the shallow water, seldom deeper than 10 feet (3 m). On one trip, ten Idaho float-tubers caught and released 118 cutthroat in four days; thirty of these weighed over five pounds.

bulging over layers of padded underclothing, and a fat goose-down parka. When I entered the lake I stepped carefully, and it was scary to wade in the dark. We had arrived by night and I had not seen the lake in daylight. My companions on this trip, who had fished the lake before, advised me: "Wade out to about hip deep and cast as far as you can. Let your line sink to the bottom and retrieve—real slow."

I had chosen a black Woolly Worm, tied on a size 4 streamer hook, with one turn of hot orange chenille at the tail and a turn of hot chartreuse chenille at the head; it had a Christmas look about it. Just as I made my first cast, I noticed the wind. In minutes, white-capped breakers stormed onto the shore, each lapping closer to the top of my waders. After dry clothes, a glorious sunrise, a snowstorm, and a hundred casts, I felt a tug at my line just as I was lifting it for a new cast. Five minutes later, a 5-lb Lahontan, dressed in gold and bronze armor, scowled at me and entered my landing net.

Pyramid Lake will reward anglers with a unique fishing opportunity for the next decade, providing that there are no setbacks such as a breakdown of cooperation between the Paiute Indian tribe and the Nevada Fish & Game Department, or some natural disaster that affects the fishing. ❧

Personal memories

I recall my first Pyramid Lake adventure as if it were yesterday. The moment my eyes fell upon the marvelous landscape surrounding the lake, and I caught my first Lahontan cutthroat with its yellow demon eyes, I was in love with the place.

How foolish I felt that first morning, walking the short distance from my room in Cosby Lodge at Sutcliffe, down to the lake in darkness when even the stars were hiding! I was wearing chest waders,

Lodging is at Sutcliffe, with snacks, groceries, gasoline and boats. Many anglers stay in Reno or Sparks, where one can find hotels, motels, casinos, restaurants and Hollywood-style entertainment.

Special fishing licenses are required by the Paiute Indian tribe. They are available at Sutcliffe.

The Green River

Dave Hughes

The Green is a long river that begins in the mountains of Wyoming and flows south through Utah and Colorado. It has 200 miles of trout water, mostly in Wyoming, and largely excellent. But the water we think of today in regard to the Green River is the 30-mile (50-km) stretch downstream from Flaming Gorge Dam, in northeastern Utah. Here the river flows through the steep, forested Red Canyon before it enters open, rolling sagebrush country.

Over 100 yards (30 metres) wide, with a deep and determined flow, the Green holds four species of trout: rainbow, cutthroat, browns, and brookies. It may have higher densities of trout per mile than any other river in the world, even if this alone does not make a dream water. Its uniqueness, besides the great numbers of fish, lies in the rich food for them and in their willingness to move for flies.

Clear water

The water is charged with nutrients from the reservoir, and the river downstream is full of scuds, small mayfly nymphs, and midges. Trout feed continually on the bottom, and rise whenever a hatch attracts them. The water in the canyon is astonishingly clear. On most rivers you spot a rising trout by the disturbance, or rise-form, it makes on the surface. But on the Green, you watch the trout itself most of the time.

A blocky black shape, sometimes in a pod of ten or even twenty, perhaps holding a foot or two under the surface, the fish spots an approaching insect and tips up slowly until its nose is out of the water, leaves some bubbles and turns down to wait for its next victim. When the light is right, you can watch the whole process. A few frustrated misses are needed before you settle down to let the trout take your fly, instead of jerking it away in fear at the sight of the black form rising toward it.

Big trout

The Green River has not always been this good. For many years it was stocked with put-and-take hatchery trout, most of them being extracted by bait fishermen before they could attain much size. In 1985, fly-and-lure-only laws were passed, with a slot limit that allows keeping two fish below 13 inches (33 cm) and only one over 20 inches (50 cm) long. This protected the medium-sized trout, and they grew rapidly because of the fine feeding. One can now cast constantly over trout of 2-3 lbs (1-1.5 kg), and see fish twice that size during a day.

There are three access points on the best part of the tailwater: Dutch John, at the base of the dam; Little Hole, about 7 miles (11 km) downstream; and Browns Park, about 20 miles (32 km) below the dam. An excellent footpath follows the upper seven miles. You can hike and fish from Dutch John, up from Little Hole, or all the way through. But this is a lot of water to cover, and the fishing is too good to cover it in a hurry.

The Green River tailwater's level can change without warning. It does not rise fast, but it can cut you off from retreat if you are already wading deep. So

you should always stay aware of where you are, and look out for any slow rise in the water level. This is easily forgotten, especially when concentrating on the trout. If you feel the water rising, head for shore at once. Anglers have been caught and drowned here.

Nymph fishing

By far the best way to fish the river is from a drift boat or raft. Floating is easy, with only one or two rapids of any dimensions. If you have any white-water experience, boating the Green is no trouble. It will bring you to lots of trout, and some people fish all day from a boat. However, I prefer to use a boat for transportation—fishing while I drift, but hopping out to wade and fish wherever the water looks good or fish are rising.

Many visitors run the upper stretch in float tubes,

a real adventure. They take lots of trout as they bob along, casting out a nymph with indicator and split shot, to be watched as it proceeds with them. Whenever they want, they can stop and stand up in the shallows, then wade and fish.

Most trout in the Green are caught on nymphs. But there are so many fish, and types of water, that you have plenty of options. You can nymph the

deep runs from a boat, get out and nymph or wet-fly fish the shallow riffles, or fish delicate dry flies over trout that feed with sipping rises on flats. The Green has it all, and offers it in beautiful surroundings.

The Green is best in spring—April through June—and again in fall, during September and October. In midsummer, the most popular water is crowded with sunbathers splashing down the river in inner tubes. This improves the view, but spoils the fishing. The lower miles from Little Hole to Browns Park are best fished in July and August. One can run into excellent midge hatches, or even mayfly hatches, whenever the weather is warm enough in winter, from November through March.

The best nymphs are No. 14-18 Gold-Ribbed Hare's Ear and No. 12-16 Olive Scuds. San Juan Worms of No. 8-12 also work well. For dries, try 16-22 Adams Midges, 18-22 Griffith's Gnats, and 16-20 Blue-Winged Olives. Since the hatches are so varied, and the fish are often choosy, you should check with fly shops at the town of Dutch John, near the river, before launching for the day. ✾

The San Juan River

Dave Hughes

A desert river in northwestern New Mexico, the San Juan is a dream water for one reason: it offers the angler an excellent chance to take a trophy trout weighing 3-6 pounds (1.3-2.7 kilograms) or even larger.

This was strictly a warm-water fishery until the Navajo Dam was completed in 1962. Rainbow trout were stocked below the dam that year, brown trout just two years later, and finally Snake River cutthroat in 1978. All of them grew quickly.

The reservoir behind the dam is 300 feet (90 metres) deep, and the outflowing river takes its water from the bottom. It emerges at a constant 45°F (7°C) all year round. The water is clear, but loaded with nutrients. Water flows are kept relatively constant, so that rooted vegetation has a chance to take hold. Consequently the streambed is rich in food for trout, which are numerous and grow abruptly. For some reason—I have heard it attributed to the cold water—San Juan trout fight harder than any trout of equal size that I have ever caught. And I haven't fished any river that supplies trout of such consistently large size. Fish from the San Juan average 3 lbs (1.3 kg) but commonly weigh 4-5 lbs, and are regularly caught in the 8-9 lbs (3.6-4.1 kg) range.

Difficult wading

This is not an easy river to fish—wide with braided channels and willow islands. The river bed is largely sand and silt, or moss-covered rock. Wading can be treacherous, and a spill in that cold water is unpleasant. Neoprene waders are necessities; a wading staff is advised. With these tools at hand, you can reach almost all of the fishable water by careful and patient wading. But you've got to feel your way, and watch out for potholes, wherever you can't see the bottom.

Fortunately, the San Juan is not subject to abrupt surges of water that take place on some tailwaters. But a hydroelectric station has been built in the last few years, so it is smart to watch the water, and to get on shore if it begins to rise while you are wading.

My favorite way to fish the San Juan is by boat. It does not make the fishing any better, or increase the numbers of fish you can catch, since access on foot to the best water is possible. But a boat does make a day on the river more pleasant, and it delivers you gracefully to water that can take a lot of effort to reach by wading. A boat also allows you to see some scenery. Since the river lies in flat sandstone country, with some interesting but far from spectacular bluffs above it, there is not much scenery to see, and you have to give yourself every chance to be pleased by it. The river is famous for its fishing, not for its beauty. In addition, a boat can·bring you to water that you may be able to enjoy by yourself, with nobody else around. The best wading water, just downstream from the dam, tends to become crowded at times.

No kill

There are no rapids on the river, and floating it is no problem even for the inexperienced. The first quarter-mile (400 metres) below the dam is designated catch-and-release only, and it attracts the highest concentration of wading flyfishermen. It also holds plenty of trout. The water is coldest there, and although the wading is not difficult, you should be extra careful not to take a tumble.

The next three and three-quarter miles (6 kilometres) are designated "quality water", and restricted to barbless flies and lures. Much of the best fly-fishing water is located in the first four miles below the dam, and most of the fishing is done there. Even those who flat the river normally finish their day at the downstream end of this short drift. There is very good fishing to keep you busy, and the many back-channels will give you some privacy.

Below the quality water, the river begins to warm up, but it takes 15-20 miles (24-32 km) to move out of the temperature ranges favored by trout. Populations of trout dwindle as you go down, but some of the biggest fish—especially cannibal browns—are caught in the miles below the quality water.

Fishing the San Juan can be condensed education. It holds so many trout that, if you're not catching any, you'll know you are doing something wrong. And it's easy to do something wrong here. Scattered hatches come off, and dry-fly opportunities exist, especially in shallow channels between islands; but the river is primarily known for its nymph fishing, which is not easy.

Nymph fishing

I fished the San Juan once with Chuck Rizuto, who is dean of guides on the river, and the best nymph fisherman I have had the chance to watch at work. As I am not a very good nymph fisherman myself, this was a real experience. His equipment was the

same as that used by most nymph fishermen: a long rod, floating line, leader as long as the rod or a bit more, a bright indicator, split shot and an un weighted nymph. The fly was fairly large, a No. 12 egg imitation.

He fished either upstream or straight downstream, in water 2-5 feet (0.6-1.5 m) deep, adjusting his indicator up and down as the depth changed, always making sure that his nymph got down deep enough to pick up some bottom moss every few casts. The amazing thing was how Chuck detected takes. San Juan trout have a reputation for taking softly and rejecting quickly, yet his indicator seemed to show nothing. Nonetheless, every once in a while he would say, "There!" and set the hook. A trout would always bounce out of the water and look around to see what had happened to it. I needed a long time to detect the tiny movements that meant a take.

The San Juan is a whole course in nymph fishing. Once you've got it down, the rewards can weigh heavily when you hold them dripping in your hand. There are enough trout in the river to let you learn quickly, since you get lots of chances. And when you learn to take trout on nymphs there, you can take them anywhere.

But you aren't likely to take larger trout on any other river, or trout so full of fight. 🪶

Lake Okeechobee

Erwin A. Bauer

A damp new day was breaking over the eastern horizon as Dick Kotis and I stowed fishing tackle and lunch into a rental boat, then cranked an ancient outboard motor until it sputtered and back-fired into life. Pulling away from the creaky dock, Dick opened the throttle and we motored out through a narrow canal. Moments later we passed through the Clewiston hurricane gate and pointed the boat northwest—across the vast expanse of Lake Okeechobee, Florida, one of the largest natural lakes in the United States. Despite the warm temperature, the spray was cold in our faces.

The 18-mile (27-km) trip from Clewiston to shallow Moonshine Bay took about an hour, and halfway there I concluded that it was worthwhile, even if we never hooked a single bass. The scarlet sunrise was that magnificent. Raft after raft of waterfowl flushed in our path and disappeared into the morning sky. Near the entrance to Moonshine Bay—named after a bootlegger who once distilled whiskey on a houseboat there—we watched an alligator slip into the water beneath a large bush heavy with roosting anhingas, locally called "water turkeys". Altogether it was (and is today) a lovely, primeval place.

A fly-box for the bass in Lake Okeechobee.

Bass on flies

The bay itself may at first disappoint an uninitiated angler. Resembling a great hayfield unevenly mowed, it has been described as "a sea of grass" and "not entirely water". Both are accurate because the cane, or grass, stretches endlessly all around, nod-

ding in the morning breeze, obscuring the water. Here and there, the grass is punctuated with patches of hydrilla, pondweed, eelgrass and lotus, all of it resembling a salad very difficult to fish.

Nearly every bass fisherman on Okeechobee normally uses bait-casting tackle, and weedless metal spoons that skitter over the dense vegetation or slither through it. This technique is very effective almost all year round. Yet my partner rigged a

heavy-duty fly rod and, to the end of a stout leader, knotted a yellow Hula Popper—a floating, popping bug with a rubber skirt tail that he had helped to design and develop. What followed was a fishing innovation I will never forget.

On his first two casts, Kotis snagged his tiny popper on vegetation. But the third fell free into a pocket of open water, and a heavy bass struck it immediately. For the next few minutes, Kotis simply held his rod high overhead as the bass wallowed and jumped all over the bay. Eventually he played it near enough for me to grasp its lower jaw, unhook and release it. The deep green bass would easily have weighed five pounds. A moment later Kotis had hooked another just like it.

Shallow water

Okeechobee has always been a very fertile fishing water. Some serious sportsmen consider it the greatest largemouth bass lake on earth—and that may be true. During the optimum season every year, from October or November until April or May, when the bass forage in shallower water, it is no trick for an average angler to hook 20-30 bass in a day's casting. More than once in years past, I have hooked twice that many. But I have never seen bass strike any lures more readily than the Hula Poppers used by Dick Kotis.

I have always wondered why more fishermen do not use fly rods at okeechobee, as so many do to catch the large bluegill sunfish on their shallow spawning beds elsewhere in winter. The ideal time to fish for bass is when they are in water 3-5 feet (1-1.5 metres) deep, according to a consensus of the most successful Okeechobee guides. If in only three feet or so, a fisherman can jump into the lukewarm water, tie the boat to his belt, and wade across the flats while casting. This is also a way to cope with the heat on very hot days. If the water is too deep to wade easily, the best strategy is to let the boat drift with the wind as you broadcast to open pockets of water all around. Edge cover, those places where two different types of vegetation meet, is productive than areas of just one kind. Areas with hard sandy bottoms are by far the best for wading and casting, or any other kind of bass fishing, since the bass seem to avoid soft and mucky bottoms. On the surface, look for lotuses: these plants, with leafpads the size of dinner plates, always indicate hard bottoms beneath.

Hunting in schools

As in many other large fertile lakes, the bass of Okeechobee sometimes gather and travel about in schools, feeding on shad. At times there are hundreds of bass feeding together, so it pays to watch for surface disturbance when you are fishing. On days when the fishing is slow, many professional guides cruise the lake until they locate such feeding bass.

Whether a small fly-rod lure snags in the thick vegetation often depends on the direction in which it was cast. So cast either with or against the wind, rather than across it. Casting upwind is more difficult, but is preferable because stems of grass will bend toward you, snagging your fly or bug much less often.

Okeechobee bass fishing requires a 9-foot, 9-weight, very stiff graphite fly rod, to deliver heavy bugs into a wind. I use a floating line and a 6-foot level leader, testing 10-12 pounds. Lighter leaders do not hold up very well against the abrasive stems of native vegetation. Bass weighing 5-10 lbs (2.3-4.5 kg) are not uncommon, and they will snap light or frayed leaders.

During the late 1980s, troubles developed at Okeechobee. A long unnatural drought, low water levels, and an algae bloom (due to run-off of fertilizer from surrounding agriculture) have caused some deterioration in fishing. Fish biologists are closely watching and studying the problem. It would be a tragedy to lose a great fishing lake such as this one.

Access to the lake is easy via numerous fishing camps and marinas at Clewiston, Moore Haven, and near Belle Glade. Complete information, guide, boat and tackle service exists at all these points. Roland Martin's Marina and Lakeside Resort at Clewiston is a complete facility that caters especially to bass fishermen. Martin himself is one of America's best-known professional bass fishermen.

The Florida Keys

Jan Olsson

The Flats in the Florida Keys belong to the world's most famous fishing arenas. Their saltwater flyfishing has been developed and refined for the past fifty years, attracting enthusiastic sportsmen from around the globe to combat some of the jumpiest, shyest and fastest species that a flyfisherman can find—the tarpon, bonefish and permit. As a classic among the sport's El Dorados, the Flats are very much alive.

Fascinating environment

About 500 islands make up the Florida Keys, forming a crescent that stretches from Miami to Key West. The car road over the coral reef between these two cities is about 120 miles (200 kilometres) long, and crosses a couple of dozen sparsely inhabited islets, much of it therefore running on bridges. These islets are also covered by mangrove swamps, like great shapeless cushions down to the water line. Flyfishing in the Keys is therefore both odd and interesting. This area was discovered at an early date by flyfishermen seeking to widen their horizons. Already in the 1920s, special tarpon flies were tied here. Local experts such as Joe Brooks and Lee Cuddy, almost half a century ago, established guidelines for flyfishing that have stood the test of time until our day.

The record lists of the International Game Fish Association (IGFA) are eloquent proof that the Florida Keys should be visited by anyone looking for easy and excellent flyfishing with light gear. Key Largo, Islamorado, Marathon, Big Pine, Key West and other names occur repeatedly in the lists every year.

A primary reason that brings flyfishermen to the Keys is naturally the shallow-water fishing, or simply "fishing over the Flats" in sportfishing parlance. It should, however, be pointed out that such fishing also exists in many other parts of the world, mainly in the Caribbean archipelago. Flats are a big shallow-water area with a clear sea and a depth that can be waded, but their character varies from place to place. The coral flats in the Florida Keys differ, for example, from the sand flats in the Bahamas, since they are largely covered by grass. This gives a fish extra camouflage and makes it harder to see. Moreover, the Florida Flats are crisscrossed by deep channels through which the fish can reach shallow water to hunt for food.

The diverse fishing here depends on the season and location. It is best during spring and autumn. In general, the closer you come to Key West in the southwest, the greater your chance of fishing all year round for the most attractive species—such as barracuda, tarpon, bonefish, permit and crevalle jack.

Ideal quarry

The most sought-after species on the Flats—bonefish, permit and tarpon—are popularly known as "the terrific trio". Taking them all on a fly rod is the dream of many a flyfisherman, and the Grand Slam of flat fishing. Millions of visitors try, but only a few have succeeded, though some have done so in a single day.

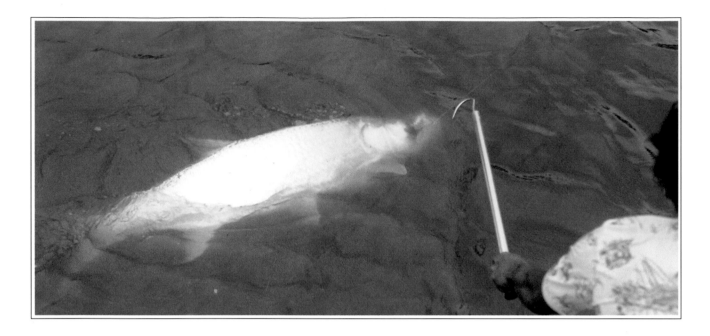

This quest is a varied one, according to the species and whether fishing is done from a boat or a shore. For the uninitiated, it is definitely easiest to rely on a guide. Otherwise the fish can be quite hard to locate, and it is extremely tiring to keep staring for them beneath the sun's glare on the water surface. Despite the crystal-clear water and the use of polaroid glasses, it may become difficult to distinguish waves from the bottom. In brief, you cannot fish as long or effectively on your own as in the company of a guide.

The boats in use, called skiffs, are 16-18 feet (4.8-5.5 metres) in length, open and very functionally built. They are well-equipped, frequently with an outboard motor of at least 100 horsepower. As a result, travel between the different flats is fast and convenient. The fishing spots are usually connected by buoyed channels and, once you reach a given spot, the motor is silenced as soon as possible. From a specially constructed platform at the stern, the guide checks the type of bottom and how the current and winds are presently moving from the deep channels toward the flats.

Then the guide stakes out a spot over the flat. The stake is around 15 feet (4.5 metres) long, and resembles a vaulting pole, conical and shod on one end and Y-shaped on the other. This mark is set up to prevent the bottom from being torn up and to avoid frightening the fish. The stake can also be used to moor the boat, if the fishing is to be done from an "anchored" position. The boat is stationed at a stone's throw from the deep channel.

Several of the shallow-water species are very sensitive and shy. Often you have only one chance to present the bait or fly, so it is essentially to move as little and carefully as possible. Normally you check in advance how the line and fly are carried by the current, and how far the casting distance is to the places where fish can be expected to appear. The latter may, for instance, be areas mashed with shrimp.

Many fishermen let the line rest in the water, ready at casting distance. When the fish exposes itself, the line is lifted quickly but cautiously, and the fly is given a strategic cast. It can then be given a few conspicuous jerks in the hope of attracting a fish.

The terrific trio

Once the fish takes, your equipment must be in trim and your nerves in order. These fish demand top preparation and an avoidance, at all costs, of problems such as old lines, sloppily tied knots, blunt hooks, mangled rod eyes, and reels with sluggish or uneven brakes.

The bonefish in the Florida Keys are popularly called "the grey ghosts of the Flats". They weigh just under 3 kg (6.6 lbs) on average, and around 9 kg (19.8 lbs) at most. Shy and incredibly speedy, a bonefish can tear 100 metres of line from your reel in a single rush. All you can do is to keep the rod tip high, rely on your gear and let the fish swim until it tires. A rod in AFTM class 6-8 is often sufficient, but the reel must be able to hold at least 200 yards of backing, besides the fly line. Bonefish come in over the flats to eat with the tide, and vanish again when it ebbs out. Their food varies with the fish's size and the flats in question, but the usual main diet is shrimp, crab, fish and octopus. Conventional streamers are used, as are familiar bonefish flies like the Bonefish Special, Honey Shrimp, Crazy Charlie, Horror, Epoxy Bonefisher and Bivisible.

Tarpon have a compressed body covered by huge scales, a sharply upturned underbite, and a bone-hard mouth cavity that makes them extremely hard to hook. They can weigh over 150 kg (330 lbs), and cruise back and forth over flat bottoms that are 1-2 metres (3-6 feet) deep, as well as in the deep channels. Generally they are fished with a rod 9-9.5 feet long in AFTM class 10-12 having a fighting butt, a top-trimmed fly reel having at least 200 yards of 30-pound Dacron backing, and a floating or sinking line—depending on the wind, current, and water depth. Since the leader is the weakest link in this equipment, the knots must be very durable. Popular

flies are the Apte Tarpon, Lefty's Deceiver, Blonde Flies, Skipping Bug, Orange Crush, Snow White and Sea Ducer, or others with orange or yellow parts.

The high-sided, silvery permit can weigh 25 kg (55 lbs), but it often appears only as a black-edged tail and back fin in clear water. It prefers somewhat deeper flats than the bonefish, with a temperature of at least 22°C (72°F), and it eats mollusks or crustaceans rather than fish. Permit are considered to be shyer and more evasive than bonefish, yet they are just as fast and definitely much stronger. This is a master of the Flats and must be approached as quietly as possible, for one very seldom gets a second chance to challenge the same fish. It requires a rod in AFTM class 9-11, and takes not only the above-mentioned bonefish patterns, but also the Brown Snapping Shrimp, Rubber-Leg Crab and Glass Minnow. These are tied on inverted hooks so that

(Left) *Tarpon can be as heavy as 150 kg (330 lbs).*

(Above) *Both permit and bonefish are notorious for their strength and speed.*

they can be fished along the bottom. ❧

Christmas Island

Steen Larsen & Jens Ploug Hansen

Boasting the world's largest atoll, Christmas Island is 50 kilometres (30 miles long). It has a lagoon about 14 km (9 miles) in diameter, populated by bonefish. The island's 1,500 inhabitants, nearly all of Polynesian origin, live on the fishing and services. It belongs to an archipelago which, together with the Gilbert Islands, has since 1977 constituted one of the world's smallest countries, the republic of Kiribati.

Kiribati and its total of 70,000 citizens are virtually unknown to the rest of the world. Christmas Island is only slightly familiar as a site of hydrogen-bomb tests in the 1950s, which luckily have not created any problems for the natives or tourists today. But in flyfishing circles, this island first drew attention during the 1980s, when it was discovered as a bonefish paradise of the Pacific Ocean. Its fishing is entirely comparable to the best in the Caribbean, and at times even better.

A dynamic fighter

Imagine yourself in a boat with a guide, who suddenly says: "Bonefish, one o'clock, 25 feet!" Your eyes scan desperately for a shadow in the transparent water, but in vain.

"Moving to two o'clock. Cast now!" he says. You glimpse the dark shape and lay out the cast. The fly lands half a yard from the fish, which zooms away in fright, leaving a little cloud of mud in the water where it disappeared. Then the guide, grinning affably, asks whether this is the first time you've been after bonefish. Your next cast places the fly half a yard from another bonefish. It is attracted, but

turns and vanishes. For almost an hour, you may cast at 10-15 of these spectres, and the same number are scared off—fish that were not noticed in time. When a bonefish finally takes the fly, your heart nearly stops. A second later you feel a click as the knot between your fly line and backing goes through the rod eyes. Before you can blink, 40-50 yards of backing are out. Once most of the line has been reeled back in again, the fish makes another rush before you can land it—and release it. In short, the rules on Christmas Island say "no kill" and require the use of barbless hooks.

That day you land a second bonefish, but lose a third, and two more cut the leader against some coral. In the afternoon, all of the flyfishermen meet on the terrace during the "golden hour", and watch a fantastic sunset across the Pacific. Your body is bur-

ning after a hard day of sunshine on the flats, and your uncovered wrists are fried red. The tropical night is warm, damp and full of noises. Sleep comes at last, and your book about Christmas Island—discovered by Captain Cook in 1770—falls to the canvas floor.

Arriving with the tide

As our experience also retells, the next day's program can be read on a big blackboard at the "Captain Cook". This is the island's only hotel, an extension of the former military base's officer quarters. It maintains fairly high standards and occupies a wonderful position, only 50 yards from the sea and surrounded by palms. You start the morning by smearing yourself with sun-cream (factor 15-24). At a water temperature of 25-30°C (77-86°F) there is no need for waders or boots, as you would soon get wet on the inside anyway. Instead, ordinary rubber shoes are used—or better still, a pair of neoprene diving shoes.

Going out through the jungle-like palm grove, you ride to the great lagoon, with its endless white coral reefs separated by turquoise-blue water. At the end of the road, you wade out into the lagoon and, helped by your guide, look for the shy bonefish that come in with the tide. Another form of fishing here is "punting" for bonefish. You are driven around in a flat-bottomed boat, or punt, about 20 feet long with a couple of 40-horsepower engines. On the way to the fishing spots, you also have a chance to trail a wobbler behind the boat: it is always possible that a barracuda or trevally might strike. A picture in the hotel bar shows a fly-caught trevally of 31 kilograms (69 pounds), so you could even get a trophy.

The fishermen are dropped off in pairs and told to cast in particular directions when the tide comes in. For the bonefish on these flats are completely dependent on the tide. They arrive in search of food, and the guides know exactly where and when to fish for them. At the Equator, a constant east wind always blows. When we got off the punt, we made sure of positioning ourselves so that the wind would be mainly at our backs. But on Christmas Island, the wind is more of a friend than a foe, since it helps to make the bonefish less shy. Besides, it dries your clothes out faster.

A bonefish takes one of your first casts, and tears 80 metres of line from the reel in a few seconds. You keep the rod high so that the line and backing stay clear of the sharp coral. When about 100 metres of line are out, the fish turns and starts to swim in

again. Reeling in the loose line as fast as possible, you think of articles and books that say a fly reel is only needed to store the line on—something you can even cut costs on!

A quarter of an hour later, you are releasing a bonefish 55 centimetres (22 inches) long, weighing 2.5 kg (5.5 lbs). By then, your hands are almost stiff

with cramps. During the next hour, your 0.30-mm leader is cut five times on the coral, but no more fish are landed. Towards afternoon, you crawl—tired and sunburned—onto the punt again, and an ice-cold beer revives you.

Typical remarks at this point are "I almost got him..." and "It was the biggest fish I ever saw!" Thus the home journey proceeds to the "golden hour" and dinner.

After some days, as Christmas Island recedes from sight 30,000 feet below your airplane, it will certainly be agreed that bonefish are dangerous for a salmon or trout fisherman. Once you have met the bonefish of that lagoon, these species will never seem as before. They're just too passive! ❧

Whoever, despite this warning, still longs to catch the bonefish in this Pacific paradise, should write to:
Frontiers
P.O.Box 161 Pearce Mill Road
Wexford, PA 15090
USA

Rio Grande

Roland Holmberg

*F*arthest south in Argentina lies one of the world's best sea-trout rivers, the Rio Grande. It flows down from the Andes through Tierra del Fuego's cold, windswept landscape to the sea. On the sides of rolling green hills graze thousands of sheep, and wild horses often appear in masses on the *pampas*.

Fishing legends

There are two different tales about how sea trout came to the Rio Grande. According to one, brown trout were implanted here—as in so many other regions—by Englishmen during the 1930s. These fish then supposedly became sea trout, by migrating out to sea and returning some years later to spawn.

The other story has it that Argentine sportfishermen, at the end of the 1930s, set out salmon and sea trout smolt which were brought from Germany. While the salmon soon disappeared, the sea trout adapted well and formed a very sturdy strain.

Which of the two versions is true, of course, is difficult to establish. Both may be partly right, or at least complementary to each other. It is certain that sea trout were implanted in the Rio Grande, and that only a small native species existed previously, which cannot have produced the sea-trout strain that now attracts flyfishermen from every continent.

At first the sea trout were not as large as they are today, and a specimen of 5-6 kilograms (11-13 pounds) was considered a real trophy. Only a few Argentine flyfishermen were then interested in the sea trout, and all of them lived at the fancy estate of

Maria Behety, which had the whole river on the Argentine side to fish from—a stretch of about 70 kilometres (44 miles). Yet gradually the fishing improved and the rumours of huge sea trout began to arise, drawing ever more sportfishermen to the Rio Grande.

Fishing in this river was made world-famous primarily by two legendary American sportfishing journalists, Joe Brooks and Ernest Schwiebert, who visited its virgin waters. Brooks fished in Argentina during the 1950s, having been invited by the government to write about the fantastic fishing and spread its reputation abroad. While on the Rio Grande, he lived at the Maria Behety, which now commands only 42 km (26 miles) of the river. Fishing guests are still accommodated in the classic English house with its heavy furniture, shiny silverware, and stewards in black/white uniforms with pomaded hair, who receive the clients and serve them at meals. However, this applies only to fishermen who are members of the family or have been invited by someone who knows the estate owner.

Ernest Schwiebert also stayed at the estate. He had read Brooks' articles, and came here to encourage luck with the sea trout that fill the Rio Grande's waters. One can hardly help feeling the wingbeats of history as one turns the pages of the old catch journal. It shows, for instance, that during four days of fishing in 1961, he landed four sea trout of 3-6 kg (6.6-13.2 lbs), though this was a lot fewer than he subsequently reported.

Violent takes

The fishing today is as good as it ever was. Some of the local estates accept fishing guests for payment, the best-known being the Kau Tapen. Its clients are mostly North Americans attracted by the lyrical writings of Brooks and Schwiebert. It controls 25 km (15 miles) of fishing water, partly bordering on that of the Maria Behety. But its water continues farther upstream, where the river is narrower and can reached more easily.

Only flyfishing is allowed on the Kau Tapen water. All sea trout must be released, in order to protect and preserve the unique strain. On average the fish weigh 3.5-4 kg (8 lbs), but every year specimens of up to 9 kg (20 lbs) are caught. Even bigger fish have been hooked, although they have usually got away. In the journal at Maria Behety, one can

condition. Usually they have small heads and thick bodies, largely because of the abundant food in the sea.

From the river mouth stretches a plateau, which is 1.6 metres (5.2 feet) deep in every direction as far as the eye can see, then dropping off to great depths. On the plateau, tidal differences of 5.5-7.3 metres (18-24 feet) occur. The fish can revel in food that ranges from tiny crustaceans to smaller fish. Scale tests have shown that the fish grow astonishingly fast.

The excellent condition of the sea trout becomes obviously when they are hooked. Their strike is violent; next they jump and rush so wildly that they seem to inhabit the air rather than the water. One finds absolutely nothing of the caution that characterizes fish in most other sea-trout rivers.

read that two fish of 11 kg (24 lbs) were caught on its stretch, and that a giant of 14 kg (31 lbs) was said to have been taken at the river's mouth, in each case with spinning equipment.

It is remarkable how many fish are caught in the Rio Grande. A mediocre flyfisherman can collect 2-5 sea trout per day with no difficulty. This is quite good, especially since the fish are shiny and in fine

Night fishing is best

The season begins in mid-January and lasts until the end of March, after which all fishing is forbidden. It is thus a comparatively short period, because the spawning occurs during April. As the season winds up, plain tendencies to spawning can be seen especially among the large male fish.

call for heavier gear is the wind, which sweeps over the river every day. But it dies down in the mornings and evenings, so there is good reason to plan your fishing at these times. Evening tends to be best, although—in contrast to most other sea-trout rivers—the fish often take poorly after dark.

While local flyfishermen customarily use almost nothing but sinking lines, it is well worth trying a floating line. To lay out a large, ample muddler in this way at dusk, and then slowly take it home, is such an exciting experience that the very thought of the results can give you the shivers! ⅔

Flies used in the Rio Grande are more reminiscent of rainbow trout flies than sea-trout flies. Black muddlers and Woolly Buggers in diverse colours have proved effective, as has General Practitioner. The local patterns are rather small and insect-like, except one named Bunny. This is nearly 10 cm (4 inches) long and consists simply of black rabbit fur wound around a single hook.

Normally a single-handed rod in AFTM class 7-9 is used. The only thing that may cause problems and

The Falkland Islands

Steen Larsen & Jens Ploug Hansen

It was as late as the aftermath of World War II that trout were implanted in the Falklands—just as they had been in South America and New Zealand, half a century earlier. The consequence today is a phenomenal sea-trout population in many rivers, as well as superb coastal fishing, on these isles of the South Atlantic. The nearest mainland is the southern tip of South America, apart from Antarctica, a couple of hours' flight from the wind-whipped Falklands.

Implanted fish

The Falklands were among the last islands in the world to be colonized. An English captain named Strong made the first landing in 1690, and during the next 150 years occasional settlements were established by the British, French, Spanish and Americans. But since 1833 the Falklands have been governed by Britain, and most of the inhabitants are therefore British, with a few Scandinavians.

Historically the main role of these islands has been to look after shipping, which—before the Panama Canal was opened—needed to go round the dreaded Cape Horn in order to reach the Pacific Ocean. However, in 1982 the Falklands became world-famous when Argentina, having long considered the islands as its own, invaded and was defeated by the British after 75 days of hard fighting.

At present about 2,000 people live in the Falklands, half of them in the town of Stanley. As the total land area is only half that of Holland, there is obviously plenty of room for both the inhabitants

and sportfishermen. The temperature is generally under 20°C (68°F), but the weather can change quite rapidly. It does not rain very much, so trees and bushes are lacking. The landscape is chiefly one of broad pastures with eroded sod and isolated cliffs—in addition to thousands of sheep.

The first British experiments with implantation involved salmon, brown trout, rainbow and brook trout, which were imported from Chile. Yet there was no success until brown trout arrived from England. In 1954 the initial catch was made of a sea trout, and proved that the English brown trout had acclimatized itself, in fact becoming an anadromous seagoing trout.

Twenty-pound sea trout

Rivers in the Falklands are not particularly large or long. The San Carlos, on East Falkland, is the longest at 45 kilometres (28 miles). Others such as the Malo, Warrah and Chartres cover 20-30 km (12-19 miles). These waters are humus-coloured as a rule, varying from fast currents to the deep calm pools where ascendant fish tend to hold.

The fish come upstream primarily during two periods: in October and November (remember that we are now in the Southern Hemisphere!), and later from February to April. Their average weight is about 2 kilograms (4.4 pounds), and a flyfisherman always makes contact with fish of 3-5 kg (7-11 lbs). Chances are also good of taking a sea trout at 5-10 kg (11-22 lbs). The record weighed 11 kg (24.2 lbs), although it was taken by spinning in the Malo River.

This fishing is largely unexplored as yet. Nobody knows just how widespread the trout are in the Falklands, since comparatively few rivers are fished. Originally sea trout were implanted at eight different places—but as time passes, the fish will probably spread to every stream and brook in the islands. Moreover, there are fine opportunities for catching trout in the lagoons or "estuaries". A surplus of krill, octopi and herring-like small fish exists, inviting the sea trout to gorge themselves. Fishing along the coasts—in fjords and bays as well as at the river mouths—is thus a rewarding kind of coastal fishing here.

Wild fighters

The wind blows almost continually in the Falklands, but counts as a challenge to seasoned casters.

Different pools are fished according to the wind direction—upstream or downstream—with single-handed gear in AFTM class 8-10. When lighter gear is used during the few lovely calm days, one soon finds that the wind was more a friend than an enemy, since the sea trout become very timid if the water surface is no longer ruffled. In contrast to many other places, sea trout here are fished in the middle of the day, for the results are so good that hardly anybody has ever tried night-fishing!

Usually the fishing is done with a floating line. Only in some spots is sink-tip or sinking line needed. The trout are by no means fastidious—orange flies of size 10-6 are effective, but black and silvery ones succeed too. Dry-fly fishing can also be practised with profit.

The Falklands sea trout is probably the strongest in the world. It has a broad, powerful body and never gives up without a real fight. Even fish that have long been in the river are more eager to take than sea trout elsewhere. This may be because so little fishing for sea trout occurs in the islands. It is not even known whether they exist in many of the rivers. Thus, one can still taste the equivocal joy of being the first in the world to fish a pool or brook, and to have it called after oneself in the annals of fly-fishing history...

But the most electrifying sport is saltwater fly-fishing in the many fjords and lagoons (estuaries). Wading about in half a metre of depth and casting at shy fish, which are waiting for rain and water in the rivers, is delightful indeed. It can become intense and hectic: for an hour one scarcely sees any fish, and then it seems as if all the sea trout intend to commit suicide by casting themselves over the flies—regardless of which patterns one has on the leader. The catch may be overwhelming, with 10-15 sea trout of 2-4 kg (4-9 lbs) in a couple of hours. One soon gets

tired and stops fishing to enjoy the natural surroundings.

Though the Falklands are a distant destination for most flyfishermen, they are unquestionably worth a visit. Daily catches of 5-10 sea trout weighing 2-3 kg (4-7 lbs) are nothing out of the ordinary. The fascinating environment, rich bird life, colonies of seals, sea lions, and sea elephants up to 5 metres (16 feet) long—together with hospitable English-speaking locals—enable one to imagine that one is in the Seventh Heaven of the Southern Hemisphere.

British Airways fly to the Falklands, and further information on the fishing is given by:

Falkland Island Tourism
Falkland House
14 Broadway, Westminster
London SW1H 0BH
England

Falkland Island Tourism
56 John Street
Stanley
Falkland Islands

Lake Taupo

Jens Ploug Hansen

Most flyfishermen are acquainted with the legendary Lake Taupo on the North Island of New Zealand. What many of us do not know is that Taupo amounts to a huge put-and-take fishing water which was created by man—and so was its ordinary fishing for rainbow and brown trout. Both species, in fact, are implanted.

Unique average weights

Taupo is 40 kilometres (25 miles) long, and up to 160 metres (525 feet) deep, covering an area of about 238 square miles. The lake was formed by a volcanic eruption 2,000 years ago. During the 1890s, the first trout fry were set out, and within a few years the lake earned a very good reputation for its excellent trout fishing. At the beginning of this century, for example, the famous big-game fisherman Zane Grey made a pilgrimage here, and caught rainbow weighing 5-8 kilograms (11-18 pounds). Thanks to his colourful, dramatic accounts of fishing in the American press, many others soon followed in his footsteps, even though it took a month by sea to reach New Zealand in those days. Before long, small sportfishing communities sprang up like mushrooms along the lake's shores, as at Turangi and Taupo. The latter had 715 residents in 1945, and today it boasts 15,000 who, as a rule, are connected with tourism and with sportfishing in particular. Lake Taupo's history is therefore unique, since the implanting of trout went so well. Between 1887 and 1907, both rainbow and brown trout were set out, but the rainbow flourished best. One registered catch from that

time shows that two fishermen took 76 trout in a single day, with an average weight of no less than 6 kg (13.2 lbs)—and seventeen of them weighed more than 8 kg (18 lbs)!

However, the fish declined rapidly in quality, as the trout soon ate the lake's entire stock of a native fish species, the "koaro". Parasites also helped to decimate the stock, and fishing became very poor during the 1920s. In the next decade, smelt were set out and saved the stock. Today they are the main food of the lake's rainbow trout.

Fishing in Lake Taupo has exploded during the last 30 years. Sales of licences numbered 10,000 in 1948-49, and 77,000 in 1983-84. A report shows that foreign sportfishermen spend a total of 502,000 days per year in the region. In 1983-84, the renowned Tongariro River—which runs into the lake at Turangi—yielded 100,082 rainbow, averaging 1.5-2 kg (3.3-4.4 lbs). During the same period, in the lake itself, four times as many were caught, meaning around 1,000 tons. This illustrates what enormous importance sportfishing and flyfishing can acquire for a community where nature and fishing are placed in a wider context.

High season in winter

Of the trout stock in the Taupo area, 70% are rainbow and the rest are brown trout. Yet in the fishing statistics, brown trout are only 2%. They are also much bigger than the rainbow, and often far harder to catch. The rainbow live an almost anadromous life, somewhat like the seagoing steelhead of the

American west coast. Every winter, from about April until August, the rainbow come up the Tongariro and several other rivers that empty into Lake Taupo, in order to spawn.

Fishing for rainbow along these rivers is best in the middle of New Zealand's winter, and reaches a zenith in June and July. Then the fish are almost all in the rivers or at their outlets. For the rest of the year, a fisherman here can find rainbow trout, brown trout that have become stationary, rainbows which have spawned and are heading out into Lake Taupo, and shiny fresh-risen fish in the larger rivers.

At Turangi, the "trout capital of the world", one can work along a 12-km (7.5-mile) stretch of the Tongariro River with its varied strength, fishing in large crystal-clear green pools, isolated little rapids and calm intervals. All year round, rainbow are

visible as they hold like dark shadows in the water, often in groups of 20-30 and weighing 1.6 kg (3.5 lbs) average. The greatest activity occurs at morning, evening and night, when the fish spread out in the water. At midday in bright sunshine, however, they gather in the shadows and the deepest channels. The few brown trout that weigh at least 3-8 kg (6.5-17.5 lbs) prefer the deepest spots and, frequently, the most obscure hideouts.

The Tongariro is only one of many rivers ascended by the rainbow trout, but it is the best-known, being accessible throughout its length. Around the lake, of course, are numerous other tributaries and it is possible to fish for several miles upstream in the biggest of them.

Flyfishing in the rivers

Until the mid-1970s, flyfishing here was generally downstream wet-fly fishing, although these rivers occasionally did offer very fine dry-fly fishing. Eventually upstream nymph fishing was developed, and this is most common today. But many visitors are still eager enthusiasts of the downstream wet-fly fishing, notably with fast-sinking or sink-tip lines.

At the river mouths, one usually finds night fishing in the warm months, when the trout approach land to enter the cooler river water. Recently, fishing with fluorescent flies has also become popular at the river outlets. The nymph fishing, especially in the Tongariro, has developed quickly. Often the fly line's outermost section, and some of the leader, are made of fluorescent line. Bite indicators are used as well—little fluorescent red, orange, or yellow foam-rubber devices, about the size of a pea. Where the indicator is fastened along the leader depends on the depth you want to fish at. But it may be at the transition between line and leader, giving a clear and certain sign of the take.

While fishing with lead weighting is not allowed in the rivers, several nymphs contain lead and copper wire. Among the most familiar are Halfback Nymph, Red Setter, Gary's Green Marabou, and Montana—or Hatepe Nymph, as the locals call it. A Pheasant Tail can also be profitable. Moreover, the sportfishing shops have an amazing range of very special nymphs invented for the region's rivers.

Some of the commonest wet flies and streamers are Mrs Simpson, Hammil's Killer, Muddler Minnow, Taupo Tiger, Parson's Glory, Fuzzy Wuzzy and Grey Ghost. In the Tongariro and the river outlets, as well as in the lake and several of its tributary brooks, there is superb dry-fly fishing at times. The main dry-fly patterns include Royal Wulff, Muddler Minnow, Dad's Favourite and Red Tippet Governor. Hatches of caddis flies and mayflies occur, and big muddlers are used as cicada imitations.

Sinking lines

Sea flyfishing is restricted to the river mouths. There, flyfishing can be done from boats—which must be anchored—over the railing and 5-15 metres (15-50 feet) out in the water. Spinning and especially trolling are practised in the lake's upper parts. Whether one is fishing from land or a boat or in waders, sinking lines are used. These are often of the extra-fast type, allowing one to fish the edges at depths of 10 metres (33 feet). Smelt imitations are common, and very effective, but perhaps less enjoyable for flyfishermen who seek elegant sporting with light equipment.

In terms of both quantity and quality, New Zealand offers some of the world's best fishing water. At Taupo and Turangi one can find guides and sportfishing shops, and the area has a wide variety of lodging—from modest houses to the "fishing lodges" that include full service and guides. Fishing licences in New Zealand cost around 20-50 U.S. dollars, depending on the region chosen. ❧

Southern New Zealand

Steen Larsen & Jens Ploug Hansen

One of the ultimate versions of trout flyfishing is "stalking trout". Nowhere else in the world can it be experienced in such demanding and refined forms as in New Zealand. It involves walking along the rivers, spying the shadows of fish, entering the water behind them, and presenting a nymph or dry fly in currents as clear as gin.

A well-deserved reputation

Many visiting fishermen have gone home disillusioned from the dream waters of New Zealand. Still more have been forced to admit that they were not quite so good at handling their fly equipment as they had believed.

On both its North and South Islands, the country has many lovely waters with trout and salmon—but the really big brown and rainbow trout are found in the pure streams and rivers along the isolated southwest coast of the South Island. These impressive fish are what have given New Zealand such a fine worldwide reputation for the sport. They are trophy quarry consisting of, on the one hand, stationary fish that live year-round in flowing water, and on the other hand, fish that undertake spawning migrations from lakes and large rivers.

A basic distinction between stalking and ordinary trout fishing is that the fish are hard to notice in the water. Even trained local fishermen can often see them only when they are frightened and flee up or down the stream. It is thus essential to wear polaroid glasses—and the New Zealand fishing literature treats stalking as synonymous with "polaroiding trout", which literally shows what the sport is about. Besides, the fishing is done only when the sun shines and no wind crosses the surface.

Quite commonly, one casts for a long time at a greyish shape on the bottom, thinking it is a fish. In the end one decides it is a stone and gives up. Suddenly it turns out to have been a fish, whose shadow is no longer there! Another important feature of this fishing is the need to place the fly exactly at the first cast. Often the water is low and crystalline, so the fish holds with no cover and is easy to scare if you make a single mistake—as though it had a third eye in the back of its head. And last but not least, you must be able to fight big fish with light equipment. With one of these large trout on your hook, it becomes a race against the clock. The longer the fish stays in the water, the greater your risk that the leader will snap or the hook come loose. Fish around 5 kilograms (11 pounds) are considered to be sizeable here, while trout of 2.5 kg (5.5 lbs) are numerous and those of 6-7 kg (13.5-15.5 lbs) count as trophies.

Flies and techniques

When stalking trout, it is often found on several of the rivers that you have to fish 5-10 kilometres (3-6 miles) of water every day—although you may make only 10-15 casts in all. The larger fish may be up to a kilometre apart, and many of them are frightened away at the first cast!

In order to cast very accurately from the outset with a small nymph, or possibly a dry fly, you need a good rod of AFTM class 4-6. Long casts are not

often required, but precise presentation is. The local patterns employed are native species of mayflies, caddis flies, stone flies and various terrestrials. As a rule, simply tied Ribbed Hare's Ear nymphs and Pheasant Tails are used. Good presentation and "induced takes" are far more important than exact patterns, but sizes 8-18 are normally chosen.

There are thousands of kilometres of trout water in the country, not all of them equally good. Yet even ignoring those with trout under 1-2 kg (2-4 lbs), huge resources remain. Many of the best waters, however, demand a willingness to walk for great distances through the bush, to use a four-wheel-drive car, or to hire an expensive helicopter. Your physique should be strong and the weather stable. Ideally it will be sunny and recently rainless, so that the water is of optimal clarity.

Rivers of the South Island

The Ahuiri, Pomahaka, Mataura, Waiangi Taona, La Fontaine, Arnold, Upper Grey and tributaries, as well as the many rivers in the Nelson district, are some of the countless big-trout waterways on the South Island, which stand in a class by themselves. Some of them are relatively suitable, being accessible by foot or a four-wheel-drive car, or at worst with a ordinary car. Perhaps best-known is the Mataura, but it chiefly yields trout of a "mere" 1-2 kilograms (2-4 lbs). The Arnold has a reputation for caddis-fly hatches and occasionally fine dry-fly fishing. The La Fontaine, at Harihari on the southwest coast, has seen both good and bad years, but is now improving again. Two other rivers of excellent character are the Pomahaka and Ahuiri.

The Pomahaka lies in the grassy highlands, an hour's travel north from Gore. This genuine wilderness river flows through deep ravines and is often diamond-clear. Its best stretches extend 15-20 km (9-13 miles) upstream from Hukaree Station. Every year fish of 4-6 kg (9-13 lbs) are landed, and there are trout of 7-8 kg (15-18 lbs). Visitors have frequently praised the Pomahaka, but like many other rivers it is difficult of access and calls for a guide, at least during a few days until one know the fishing conditions.

Despite the inexhaustible appearance of New Zealand's rivers and its trophy trout, the big fish are limited in number, and the trophies are not replaced in many of the waters. Indeed, although few admit it, there is an effective and widespread—though forbidden—practice of net-fishing in several of the rivers, which has decimated the stocks of large trout.

The Ahuiri flows through a quite different sort of landscape, near the village of Omarama in the province of Canterbury. Starting in the mountains, it traverses one of the South Island's most beautiful areas—the Ahuiri Valley—down to the village and onward to Lake Benmore, which is extremely rich in fish. Here the classic fishing takes place above the "first" and "second" forest huts. These small overnighting cabins can be used at almost no cost. The river is comparatively wide and varies from deep pools to broad stretches. At one famous beat, the Horseshoe Lagoon below the first forest hut, fish of 5-6 kg (11-13 lbs) often hold. Farther up, your chances are better; With favourable conditions it is not unusual to find fish of that size, and to hook a few trout of at least 2-3 kg (5-7 lbs).

Below Omarama, the river is more accessible, though the fish are smaller and equally shy. A guide

is often necessary until you are familiar with the conditions. This river has been sensational during recent seasons, and is undoubtedly one of the world's leading big-trout waterways. ✲

Index